Opening Doors
of Truth and Love

20 TEEN PRAYER SERVICES

20
TEEN PRAYER SERVICES

Opening Doors of Truth and Love

S. KEVIN REGAN

TWENTY
THIRD 23rd
PUBLICATIONS

Dedication

To my grandchildren,
Aidan, Andrew, Aimee, and Benjamin

Chapter 4, pp.18: Story adapted from an article that appeared in *The Providence Visitor*, the newspaper of the Diocese of Providence, RI.

Chapter 8, pp.37-38: Story adapted from *Modern Spirituality: An Anthology*, edited by John Garvey; Templegate Publishers.

Chapter 9, pp.41-42: Story adapted from *Quips and Quotes and Anecdotes*, Edited by Anthony Castle; Twenty-Third Publications.

Twenty-Third Publications
A Division of Bayard
185 Willow Street
P.O. Box 180
Mystic, CT 06355
(860) 536-2611 or (800) 321-0411
www.twentythirdpublications.com
ISBN:1-58595-509-4

Library of Congress Catalog Card Number: 2004117874
Printed in the U.S.A.

Contents

Introduction

The new millennium is now upon us. The challenges it places before religious educators and those working with young people in the Church are immense. The statement made in Montreal in the year 2001 by the Brothers Visitor of the Americas (De La Salle Christian Brothers) expresses well a summons for each of us: "We call on our Church to recognize with us that the young people of our hemisphere and our world are searching for God and for a lived witness to the gospel of Jesus Christ." This book is a response to that challenge. It is an attempt to help those ministering to youth share their search with the teens they serve and teens bear witness to the gospel of Christ.

Praying with teens and *for* teens is a primary way to witness to the gospel. Thomas Merton reminds us that prayer is, first of all, life! The life of teens takes them to the sought-after harbor of adulthood only by crossing over the turbulent waters that so often accompany adolescence. They travel in a world linked by computers, divided by war, united in efforts to overcome injustice, and separated by huge chasms of economic, political, and social inequality. While many people throughout the world suffer lives of hopelessness and misery, others enjoy multiple opportunities for interesting careers, material wealth, and travel. This landscape forms the real world, the local and global neighborhoods for the young people we serve.

For the catechist or religious educator, only two doors open into the lives of teenagers. One is the door of truth and the other is the door of love. This resource is meant to assist you—youth ministers, catechists, religious educators, campus ministers, and retreat directors—in opening those doors in your own lives and in the hearts and minds of those you serve. The stories, prayers, questions, quotations, and readings from Scripture are meant to support you in your efforts to bring Christ's love to the lives of teenagers while helping them bring their desires, hopes, and fears to their loving God.

The themes presented here are those with which teenagers are most familiar and offer them the most persistent challenge: self-identity and uniqueness, friendship and community, the lure of alcohol and other drugs, sexuality and love, death and grieving, prayer and listening, care for the environment, violence and peacemaking, poverty and service, vocation and dreams, to name a few. Conversation with God in prayer offers a privileged opportunity to teach the way of discipleship and to reinforce gospel truths. This awareness is woven throughout these prayer services. Leaders are encouraged to use appropriate music to accompany and enhance the prayer experience.

Each prayer service is organized in the following fashion:

Times for Use offers suggestions for occasions when the prayer services would be appropriate. When possible, the themes match with feasts from the liturgical year.

Introduction welcomes participants with an introduction to the theme of the prayer service. The prayer leader can use the quotations, questions, and suggested activity to help participants focus on the theme.

Call to Prayer invites an awareness of God's presence. Through the focus prayer, those gathered are joined to the mercy and love of God. This prayer can be used independently or as a beginning or ending prayer for a youth gathering related to the theme.

Scripture Reading introduces and expresses the theme as found in God's word.

Pause allows silent reflection on the Scripture reading.

Reflection provides a story for the prayer leader or presider to share. The presider may also substitute his or her own story as a way to offer witness to the gospel. One or more of the young people can do this as well.

Quiet Time allows reflection on the ideas that were shared.

Response allows the young people to answer God's word in vocal prayer or action. The response also encourages the young people to continue reflecting and acting on the theme of the prayer service.

The prayer services can be effectively used in various ways. The services may all be used as they appear, but the format also allows flexibility for the creativity of the organizer(s) of the prayer service. The specific needs of a particular community and local circumstances may be a primary factor in determining the form the services will take. Above all, the goal is to encourage young people to pray by offering them a reverent, theologically sound, and an aesthetically beautiful experience of prayer.

CHAPTER 1

The Gift of Faith

Celebrating Our Catholic Identity

Times for Use
- Preparation for Confirmation
- Theme: what a Catholic believes
- Feast of All Saints

Introduction

Leader

The Catholic identity for a pre-Vatican II Catholic was expressed in part in a common language for Mass, a specified habit of dress for women and men religious, a shared understanding of the faith passed on by the *Baltimore Catechism*, and an authority that was expressed through a hierarchical structure. The Second Vatican Council initiated significant changes, and the liturgical movement begun before the Council bore fruit in Council decrees. Biblical research led to the encouragement of an understanding of the historical, cultural, linguistic, and theological origins of the Bible. A new age of ecumenism was born.

The Church declared the right of each person to religious freedom even as it expressed a new relationship to non-Christian religions. War was to be evaluated with an entirely new attitude and the Pastoral Constitution of the Church in the Modern World (*Gaudium et Spes*) identified the Church with the struggles and hopes of people everywhere. A mantra often heard after the Council was, "The people are the Church."

Today we reflect on our Catholic identity. There is a mystery at the center of our individual identities and at the center of the Church's identity as the Mystical Body of Christ. We might ask ourselves how we would answer the question, "What does it mean to be a Catholic Christian?"

Call to Prayer

Leader   Let us remember we are in the holy presence of a loving God. God the Creator, Jesus our Savior, and Spirit of truth all holy, we come to you in prayer to deepen our understanding of our Catholic identity and to celebrate its vitality and vision. We pray with both gratitude and awe for such a life-changing, hope-filled gift.

All   Amen.

Scripture Reading

Leader   Our Catholic identity is expressed in our shared faith, as stated in the Nicene Creed and the Apostle's Creed. Our faith is celebrated in the Eucharist and the seven sacraments. Our faith is lived by following Christ's law of love expressed in Scripture, and the dynamic, living tradition of the Church. Our life in Christ is experienced in prayer, in service, in eucharistic celebration, in union with God. Our Scripture reading sees with the eyes of Christ that love is the flash point of faith, the light that beckons all people to see that the truths of the Catholic faith are not far away and abstract but dynamically present in the faith-filled living of daily life.

Reader   A reading of the gospel according to John. (John 15:9–14)

Pause

Reflection

Use this story, adapt it, or substitute your own story or reflection to suit your needs.

There is a story told about author Robert Louis Stevenson. As a small boy in Scotland, Robert used to sit at dusk near a window in his house that overlooked the town. As he watched intently, a lamplighter would approach the street lamps and light each one individually. One evening Robert's mother watched with interest her son's attention to the work of the lamplighter. She inquired of him, "Robert, what are you doing?" He paused and looked over his shoulder. Full of the childlike wisdom praised in the gospel reading he said, "Mother, I am watching a man who punches holes in the darkness."

Both the gospel story and the words of the young author to his mother tell us something important about our Catholic identity. Jesus reminds us that we become the people God calls us to be by remaining in his love. We believe in a God who is in a relationship of love, the Holy Trinity. Through union with Jesus we become one in this great mystery of God's love. Our Catholic identity then, is something concrete and real. It means living our daily lives from our relation to God. In the words of Edith Stein, St. Theresa Benedicta of the Cross, "it is to love Christ above all things, not only in mind and heart but in the exercise of daily life."

Above all, our Catholic identity sees each event in life through the eyes of faith. In this way we punch holes in the darkness of a world that often sees the world as incomprehensible, a prison of space and time ending in death. Faith transcends time uniting the seasons of one's life to the timeless joy of eternal life. Faith overcomes the separation and incompleteness imposed by the limits of space through union with Christ, by which human love is united to divine love. What is begun here in an incomplete and imperfect manner is brought to its sought-after end. The story of our longing for a home and complete acceptance ends in the total satisfaction of God's embracing love. Union quiets the longing of the mind for absolute truth. The adventure of the human pilgrimage reaches its desired destination: God's unconditional love.

Quiet Time

Response

Pass out paper and pencils. Invite the teenagers to complete the following statements printed on their papers: My beliefs about God are…I believe…I celebrate my faith in God by…I follow Jesus by…I live my beliefs by…I pray by…I experience closeness to God when I…. Invite them to share in groups of two, with selected responses offered to the whole group. Because divine mystery is at the center of faith, questions, doubt, paradox, or ambiguity can be expected in some responses. A brief discussion may follow.

Continue the response with a profession of faith. As the profession is being made a large candle will be carried to the front of the congregation and placed in a candleholder. Give each participant a small candle to be lighted from the large candle.

Leader	Let's respond to our reflection on our Catholic identity by sharing a profession of faith. We will pray the Nicene Creed slowly in a choral fashion.
Left Side	We believe in one God, the Father, the Almighty, maker of heaven and earth, of all that is seen and unseen.
Right Side	We believe in one Lord, Jesus Christ, the only Son of God, eternally begotten of the Father, God from God, Light from Light, true God from true God, begotten not made one in Being with the Father.
Left Side	Through him all things were made. For us and for our salvation he came down from heaven: by the power of the Holy Spirit he was born of the Virgin Mary and became man.
Right Side	For our sake he was crucified under Pontius Pilate; he suffered, died, and was buried.
Left Side	On the third day he rose again in fulfillment of the Scriptures; he ascended into heaven and is seated at the right hand of the Father. He will come again in glory to judge the living and the dead, and his kingdom will have no end.
Right Side	We believe in the Holy Spirit, the Lord and giver of life, who proceeds from the Father and Son. With the Father and Son he is worshipped and glorified. He has spoken through the prophets.
Left Side	We believe in the one holy catholic and apostolic Church. We acknowledge one baptism for the forgiveness of sins. We look for the resurrection from the dead and life in the world to come.

All   Amen.

The leader now invites all participants to join hands as the following blessing is offered.

Leader   God the Creator, Jesus the Savior, and Holy Spirit the life giver, bless those gathered here who profess faith in you. Help us to say yes to your invitation to be people of faith. Guide us to action that seeks to establish justice and serve your poor. Lead us to a deepened awareness of your holy presence that we may sing your love song and step and turn to your dance of peace for all of your creation. As these candles shed light on us, may our faith in you bring light to our world. We pray to you, loving God in Christ and by the power of his Holy Spirit.

All   Amen.

Candles can now be safely extinguished.

CHAPTER 2

Who Is My Neighbor?

Being a Good Samaritan in the New Millennium

Times for Use
- Feast of St. Martin de Porres
- Thanksgiving
- Retreat on the theme of mission

Introduction

Leader

The single greatest challenge to the gospel of Jesus Christ today is the poverty that destroys the lives and the hopes of millions of God's people. According to the UN 2003 Human Development Report, fifty-four countries are poorer now than they were in 1990. Women often bear the greatest weight of poverty. Thirty-five thousand children die daily from hunger and preventable diseases. According to the Maryknoll Office for Global Concerns, 840 million people in the world are malnourished and 153 million of them are under the age of five.

Theologian Gustavo Gutierrez shares a powerful insight when he says, "Neighborhood is a result of commitment and not of place." He clearly states the challenge poverty poses for the Catholic Christian: "The poor worldwide are dying before their time, and they are dying a different kind of death. The death is still physical but more so today, it is cultural. Their dignity is denied and they are not respected. This is a kind of death. If we see poverty in this broader context, we can understand grinding poverty as exactly contrary to the will of God because the gift of God is life….Resurrection is the victory of life over death while poverty simply means death. I think this is so because the root of poverty is the refusal to love….Here, as elsewhere, the only sin is not to love."

This prayer service places the parable of the Good Samaritan at the center of a world in which the gap between rich and poor is a scandal to those who follow Jesus' gospel. Because it is the young who are most frequently the victims of poverty, it is appropriate that young people pray to be empowered by God to help create a more just society. We pray then for a new Pentecost, that God's spirit renew in us the awareness of our call as disciples of Jesus Christ to stand with the poor in ways that support their efforts to claim those basic necessities central to human dignity.

Call to Prayer

Leader	Let us remember we are in the holy presence of a loving God. In the name of the Father,
All	Who freed the Jewish people from slavery in Egypt;
Leader	And of the Son,
All	Who brings liberty to the oppressed and sets captives free;
Leader	And of the Holy Spirit,
All	Who raises the lowly to high places and fills the hungry with good things. Amen.

Scripture Reading

Leader	In our world of instant global communications, the question asked of Jesus, "Who is my neighbor?" has global consequences. Aware of our new situation we listen to the answer offered to each of us by Jesus.
Reader	A reading from the gospel according to Luke. (Luke 10:25–37)

Pause

Reflection

The young girl stood shyly looking down. Her name was Lisa Rahman, and she was from Bangladesh. Dressed in a sari, she stepped up to the microphone. Lisa had been in the United States for weeks, speaking throughout the country. She was homesick for her country but she had to speak for the women of Bangladesh. Beginning at age thirteen, these women work for twelve hours a day in sweatshops to make clothing. Speed of the work, beatings, the work schedule, and sub-standard wages keep Lisa and others like her entrenched in poverty. Lisa has asked for one day a week off and a wage of thirty-seven cents an hour, instead of seven cents an hour.

In places like Mexico, Central America, Southeast Asia, and China women work as many as twelve hours a day for five dollars a day. Much of the clothing made in sweatshops is sold in the United States. Disney, Wal-Mart, and other well-known companies have been asked to admit they sell clothing made in sweatshops and to offer a fair wage and safe working conditions for those who work in sweatshops. Groups of high school students have formed throughout the country to support the efforts of people like Lisa.

As we reflect on the gospel, do we consider Lisa and those working in sweatshops throughout the world to be our neighbor? Is neighborhood a matter of commitment or a matter of place?

Quiet Time

Response

Our first response to God's words might be to identify local poverty. Perhaps it is the unemployed, the underemployed, the homeless, single parents, children, or the elderly poor. Next, the young people could suggest ways that they can help those people living in poverty to overcome their present circumstance. Invite participants to write prayers of petition in small groups around the theme, "God hears the cry of the poor." One person from each group can read their prayer of petition. The response is, "Give us ears, O God, to hear the cry of the poor." If time does not permit, the following may be used.

Leader	We have heard the words of the gospel directed at us. We know that our neighbor is anyone, anywhere, who is in need. We pray that we may hear and answer their call to us.
Pray-er One	When the poison of poverty destroys the lives of your people, we pray,
All	Give us ears, O God, to hear the cry of the poor.
Pray-er Two	When profits are put before people, we pray,
All	Give us ears, O God, to hear the cry of the poor.

Pray-er Three	When homelessness, unemployment, and lack of health care plague your people, we pray,
All	Give us ears, O God, to hear the cry of the poor.

The papers with prayer petitions may be presented to the leader. Continue with the prayer.

Pray-er Four	Loving God, you hear the cry of the poor. When the poison of poverty attacks the human dignity of your people,
All	May we be the neighbor who cares for your poor.
Pray-er Five	Your prophets call us to live just lives. Your son, Jesus, came to proclaim liberty to captives, release to prisoners and to open the eyes of the blind.
All	We pray that you stir up a new Pentecost in our midst, that we might work untiringly for a more just society and we may be the neighbor who cares for your poor.
Pray-er Six	Accept, O God of justice, the actions listed on these papers and help us to carry them out. We pray in Jesus' name,
All	May we be the neighbor who cares for your poor.

All are invited to stand shoulder to shoulder.

Leader	We thank you for the lives we live. Help us to show our gratitude to you by standing in solidarity with those suffering from poverty just as we stand now shoulder to shoulder. Help us to be a true neighbor to those in need.
All	Amen.

CHAPTER 3

Mary's Yes

Courage and Consequences

Times for Use
- Feast of the Annunciation
- Retreat on the gifts of the Holy Spirit
- Celebration around the themes of courage and responsibility
- Presentation on the importance of saying, "yes" or "no"

Introduction

Leader

A French proverb says, "To a brave heart nothing is impossible." People who develop brave hearts will overcome the challenges posed by the new millennium. Some of the greatest acts of courage take place in the very ordinary circumstances of daily life. Mary's "yes" to the angel who asked her to become the mother of Jesus is one example. Mary never planned to change all of human history. Her only intention was to do God's will. If we say "yes" to God with our talents and abilities, and if we bring new ideas and energy to our broken world, imagine the good God can do through us! Mary's example and that of many people who courageously accept heavy burdens each day raise some important questions: What is courage? What is responsibility? How do I develop the gift of courage in my life? How can I become a more responsible person?

Call to Prayer

Leader   Let us pause to remember that we are in the holy presence of a loving God. Mary, when you were still a young girl, you were asked to become the mother of Jesus. The invitation must have filled you with fear and anxiety. You could have said no. Your courageous "yes" to God changed forever both your life's direction and the course of human history. We will make your prayer to God our own: "Let it be done to me according to your word." We pray to you, Holy Spirit, counselor and advocate. We seek the wisdom to know the power of the words "yes" and "no." Guide us to find the courage to accept the consequences of our decisions. We pray this in the name of Jesus, son of Mary and son of God.

All   Amen.

Scripture Reading

Leader   Today we celebrate the feast of the Annunciation. On this day we remember the visit of the angel Gabriel to Mary, to tell her that she would become the mother of Jesus. Although she was a poor young girl who lacked the trappings of power and prestige that surround the rich and powerful today, Mary said "yes" to God. Her "yes," her absolute trust in God changed history for all time. Today we celebrate Mary's "yes" and we honor all those people who say "yes" to God each day. This feast is a reminder of the power attached to the words "yes" and "no." To say "yes" means we accept all the consequences of our decision. We know this will often take great courage for us as it did for Mary.

Reader   A reading of the gospel according to Luke. (Luke 1:26–38)

Pause

Reflection

The story of Mary's "yes" to God reminds me of the story of Cathy, a young girl about your age. The story was in a local newspaper. At the beginning of her first semester her life was on course to a great senior year topped off by graduation celebrations. She shared many of the concerns of people her age. She worried about grades and getting into college after graduation. As a star athlete she looked forward to the soccer, basketball, and softball seasons.

Cathy's life was turned upside down when her mother died of cancer. Now she was faced with some very serious choices. She took responsibility for her younger brother, a sister, and her nephew, adapted her desires to the new circumstances. Cathy said "no" to some of her wants in order to say "yes" to unexpected needs that her mother's death placed in her young hands. Her "yes" changed forever the lives of her brother, sister, and nephew.

Like, Mary, Cathy said "yes" to God by responding in a courageous and responsible way to the needs of those around her. For both Mary and Cathy saying "yes" to God meant accepting new responsibilities while saying "no" to their own wants and desires.

Now is a wonderful time to reflect on our own ability to say yes and no. Can we back up our words with responsible behavior? Do we have the courage to do the right thing, the responsible thing, even when others and our selfishness encourage us to take the easy way out of difficult situations?

Quiet Time

Response

Hang a picture of the Madonna and child where all can see it. Light candles. If possible, pass out holy cards with a picture of the Madonna. Ask the young people to look at their card and decide what was courageous about Mary's "yes" to God. Remind them of her age and circumstances as a young girl living in Nazareth. Ask them: If they were in Mary's position, what they would be concerned about? Have them list the qualities that make a person courageous on posterboard. Individually or in small groups, invite the teens to create a prayer for some friend who needs God's help at the present moment. These prayers may be written on one side of a card; the other side of the card can be decorated. When everyone is finished, continue with the prayer service.

Leader	We gather on this feast of Mary to honor Mary by praying to God through her son. Our response will be, "We say 'yes,' my Lord."
Pray-er One	Mary said "yes" and accepted all the responsibilities her words contained. Lord, when we are faced with the unwanted responsibilities that come from our choices,
All	We say "yes," my Lord.
Pray-er Two	Lord, when we turn from the consequences of our decisions and escape from the situations we have created, we accept our responsibility,
All	We say "yes," my Lord.

Pray-er Three	Sometimes we forget the power we hold by using the words "yes" and "no." Lord, we can use these words carelessly and harm other people in a lasting way. But we can also be aware of the power of our words,
All	We say "yes," my Lord.

Invite the teenagers to share their prayers with the larger group at this time. The service then concludes.

Leader	Our response will be a choral recitation of the Magnificat. This is the great prayer by which Mary celebrates her union with God.
Pray-er Four	Gentle God, through the yes of Mary, Jesus became one of us. His mother's love formed his view of life and taught him responsibility and courage. We thank you for Mary and pray that we may learn from her example. We pray, too, for all those people, especially people our age who are courageously carrying adult responsibilities because they said yes to life around them. We too share in Mary's joy as we pray,
Left Side	My soul proclaims the greatness of the Lord and my spirit rejoices in God my Savior;
Right Side	For he has looked upon his servant in her lowliness: all ages to come shall call me blessed.
Left Side	God who is mighty has done great things for me, holy is his name;
Right Side	His mercy is from age to age on those who fear him.
Left Side	He has shown might with his arm; he confused the proud in their inner most thoughts.
Right Side	He has deposed the mighty from their thrones and raised the lowly to high places.
Left Side	The hungry he has given every good thing, while the rich he has sent away empty.
Right Side	He has upheld Israel his servant, ever mindful of his mercy;
Left Side	Even as he promised our fathers, promised Abraham and his descendents forever.
All	Amen.

CHAPTER 4

The Gospel Has a Heartbeat

Following Christ's Way of Peace

> **Times for Use**
> - The theme of peacemaking
> - The theme of world peace
> - World Peace Day—January 1st
> - Ash Wednesday and the beginning of Lent

Introduction

Leader

A song by John Lennon says, "Give peace a chance." But what is peace? Peace is not the absence of war but an enterprise of justice. Peace is not one person, one economic system, or one country dominating another. Peace has been described as the tranquility of order. Part of seeking justice and establishing order in the world is to consider our attitude toward war.

The Second Vatican Council says that we are, "to evaluate war with an entirely new attitude." What is that new attitude? Do we believe, with Pope John Paul II, "War is a defeat for humanity. Only through peace, in peace, can respect for human dignity and its inalienable rights be guaranteed." Human dignity demands justice; the common good demands that human rights be protected. Are we convinced that war is a human creation, and that humans can find more rational and human ways to establish peace? Is the abolition of war as a means to solve conflict a goal we embrace?

The challenges to justice and peace in the new millennium are already upon us. Peace truly begins with each one of us. It is important to reflect on what God is asking of us as disciples of Christ. Are we trying to become peacemakers in this culture of violence? Some helpful questions are: What is peace? Am I at peace with God? How am I a peacemaker at school, in my home, and in the other communities to which I belong? Can Lent be a time to work at learning the methods of peacemaking in order to confront the violence within the world?

Call to Prayer

Leader   Let us remember we are in the holy presence of a loving God. God of Peace, you invite us during this holy season to turn from ways of injustice and violence to the ways of peace. The gospel challenges us to repent and believe the Good News. Help us to discipline our minds to learn the methods of peacemaking and to guide our wills to choose what is good, what is just. We pray this in union with Jesus, the peacemaker, and by the power of the Holy Spirit.

All   Amen.

Scripture Reading

Leader   With Ash Wednesday we begin another season of Lent. Lent is a time of pilgrimage, a journey from the ashes that remind us of our earthly fate, to the Paschal Candle that lights our minds and strengthens our wills with the knowledge that we are an Easter people. We are people of the resurrection, and alleluia is our song! The journey through Lent is taking place while, somewhere in the world, war is being waged. Lent invites each of us to a change of heart, a conversion to live the gospel way, Christ's way. War and our participation in it directs us to pause, to pray, to study, to fast, and to act. Let's listen together to Christ's words to us his followers.

Reader   A reading from the gospel according to Matthew. (Matthew 5:43–48)

Pause

Reflection

This story, which comes from South Africa, is one recent example of how the gospel transforms people's lives today. The scene is a courtroom in South Africa. A seventy-year-old black woman slowly stands. Opposite her are white security officers. One of the officers, Mr. Van der Broek, was found guilty of killing the woman's son and burning his body while Van der Broek and his comrades partied. He later returned and took the woman's husband; two years later, he came for the woman. She was taken to a spot where her husband was tied, beaten, and lying on a pile of wood. As the officers poured gas over him and set fire to him the man responded, "Father, forgive them."

Mr. Van der Broek confessed to these crimes. The judge faced the woman and asked how justice could be done to this man who so brutally destroyed her family? "I want three things," responded the woman. "I want first to be taken to the place where my husband's body was burned so that I can gather up the dust and give his remains a decent burial. My husband and my son were my only family. I want secondly, therefore, for Mr. Van der Broek to become my son. I would like him to come twice a month to the ghetto and spend a day with me so I can pour out on him whatever love I have remaining within me. And, finally, I want a third thing. I would like Mr. Van der Broek to know that I offer him my forgiveness because Jesus Christ died to forgive. This was the wish of my husband. And so I would kindly ask someone to come to my side and lead me across the courtroom so that I can take Mr. Van der Broek in my arms to embrace him and let him know he is truly forgiven."

At this point Mr. Van der Broek fainted and friends, family, and neighbors in the courtroom began singing, "Amazing grace how sweet the sound that saved a wretch like me."

The gospel instructs us to love our enemies, to do good to those who hate us, and to bless those who curse us. We might rather skip these words or water them down to be less demanding, but they are the heart and the heartbeat of the gospel. Peace is both a gift from God and a human work. The gospel encourages us to read, to learn, and to study ways to solve conflict that do not involve violence. It asks us to see from God's perspective, and when it comes to war, to "evaluate war with an entirely new perspective." Our attitudes, thoughts about others, and decisions about how to resolve conflict in our lives will create the world we will inhabit in the future. Let us pray for one another that, like the woman in the story, we may follow the way of peace and forgiveness, the way of Jesus which alone offers hope for our world.

Quiet Time

Response

A lighted candle will be placed on a table in front of the assembly. Small paper doves may be cut out ahead of time and arranged around the place of prayer, one for each person. If time permits, they can make their own. Next, encourage those present to reflect on the gospel and the story. Ask them to write on the paper the name of a person who gives them a hard time, someone they may dislike. On the other side of the paper, invite the young people to write one thing they could do to encourage peace with the person they named. As an alternate, they could name one thing they could do to bring peace into their homes, schools, or the larger world.

After the shared response at the end of the first prayer, have a few young people bring the papers up and place them on the table in front of the lighted candle. Holy cards with the Prayer of St. Francis can be placed on the altar or table. If possible, those participating could stand around the altar or table.

Leader	The response is, "God of justice, with your help we will become instruments of your peace." During Lent we are invited to pray, to fast, and to give to those in need. By these actions we become less selfish and free to love more completely those people God has placed in our lives. Together let us renew our commitment to become peacemakers and to live peaceful lives.
Pray-er One	Loving God, you invite us to love all people. We ask you to heal in us any bias, any prejudice, or any need to be right. We know that these can lead to violence in our relationships with others. For our part we promise;
All	God of justice, with your help we will become instruments of your peace. *Place written responses next to the candle.*
Reader One	God of peace, we commit ourselves to the task of overcoming prejudice in our lives. We further promise to make room in our hearts for other people even those who disagree with us. This Lent we will give up the need to always be right. May you bless our efforts to be instruments of your peace.
All	Amen.
Pray-er Two	Loving God, if we are filled with conflict within ourselves, we cannot bring peace into our world. We know the music we listen to, the movies and videos we watch, influence our thoughts and feelings. You desire order within our minds and imaginations. For our part we promise;

All	God of justice, with your help we will become instruments of your peace. *Place written responses next to the candle.*
Reader Two	God of peace, we promise this Lent to monitor the songs videos and television shows, which usually fill our eyes and ears. We will try to replace the violence and disrespect of some media with entertainment that nourishes the values and goals of peacemaking. May you bless our efforts to be instruments of your peace.
All	Amen.
Pray-er Three	Loving God, peace is not the absence of violence nor is it the experience that everything in our world is on track. Peace is the gift of shalom, inner harmony, order, and justice in society. Peace is another word for justice that treats people throughout the world with dignity and respect. For our part we promise;
All	God of justice, with your help we will become instruments of your peace.
Reader Three	God of peace, we promise this Lent to try to be fairer in our relationships with each other. We also commit ourselves to the work of becoming aware of injustice in our schools, in our local communities and in the larger world. May you bless our efforts to become instruments of your peace.
All	Amen.
Pray-er Four	Loving God, peace often escapes us because we refuse to think and act like people who value peace. Only through the peace that is built on our relationship with you can we bring peace into the world in which we live. For our part we promise;
All	God of justice, with your help we will become instruments of your peace.
Reader Four	God of peace, we promise this Lent to set aside a few minutes each day to pray to you for peace in our hearts and in our world. We will meet you more often at the table of the Eucharist so Christ can fill us with his love, which is the source and end of all peace. May you bless our efforts to become instruments of your peace.
All	Amen.
Leader	We will close our service tonight by praying together the Prayer of St.

Francis. As you pray you think of that person with whom you need to make peace.

Say the Prayer of St. Francis. Participants may then share the Kiss of Peace. Encourage all to read the Prayer of St. Francis each day during Lent. If the holy cards are not available the following may be used as a closing.

Pray-er Five	God of peace, God of justice, breathe your Holy Spirit of love and courage into us this Lent. Help us united with Jesus to confront violence in all its forms.

Invite participants to name the person with whom they find it difficult to be reconciled.

Pray-er Five	Renew us during Lent with a joy in your presence and the conviction that you are with us always to help us to love those who may not love us. Remind us whatever we do to the least of our sisters and brothers we do to you. We pray this in union with Christ the peacemaker, our Lord and brother and by the power of Holy Spirit.
All	God of peace, with your aid we will become instruments of your peace.
Leader	You are the God of peace and the strength of peacemakers everywhere. Peace is both your gift and human work. Help us to dedicate ourselves each day to the work of peace. May we look for the gift of your grace, your holy presence as we work to overcome injustice and we seek to establish the reign of Christ on earth. We pray this through Christ the peacemaker, and by the power of the Holy Spirit of peace.
All	Amen.

CHAPTER 5

When Grief Knocks on Our Door

Surviving the Death of a Friend

Times for Use
- All Souls Day
- At the time of a death
- At a healing service
- Retreat theme of grief and new life

Introduction

Leader　　How do we cope with death? How do we deal with the losses that come into our lives? A student said recently, "If you open your heart to someone, you have to go through suffering." It is all too common to discover that a friend has died in a car accident or a grandparent has succumbed after battling cancer or some other disease. The pain of divorce marks another loss, a kind of death that many must face today.

It is especially at these times that we are shocked by the harshness of life. We are forced sometimes at a very young age to confront loss and to search for meaning in the mystery of human suffering and death. We come together in prayer to help one another confront the experience of loss and the suffering it forces upon us.

Call to Prayer

Leader	Let us remember that we are in the holy presence of a loving God.
Pray-er One	God of sorrow, God of hope, Jesus experienced anguish at the death of his friend, Lazarus. He wept over the city of Jerusalem and the suffering that was to visit her people. He was in agony over the thought of his own death.
Pray-er Two	But Jesus brought three gifts to the mystery of death to strengthen us in our sorrow. He promised he would be with us in our suffering through the love of the Christian community. He promised that our suffering, which unites us with all who suffer, could be redemptive, that it could bring healing to our world. Jesus also promised that earthly death is not a final end to our identity, but a passage into new life, the completion and fulfillment of our heart's desire.
Pray-er Three	God of hope, we turn to you now to ask you to help us to mourn our losses and to deepen our faith in the resurrection from the dead. We pray this through Christ, our Lord,
All	Amen.

Scripture Reading

Leader	In our Scripture passage we see Jesus mourn the loss of his friend, Lazarus, and comfort Lazarus' family. By God's power Jesus brings Lazarus back to this life as a sign of his own resurrection into eternal life and a promise of our own.
Reader One	A reading of the gospel according to John. (John 11:1–7, 11–44)

Because of the length of this passage, three readers can be used.

Reader One	John 11:1–7
Reader Two	John 11:11–27
Reader Three	John 11:28–44

Pause

Reflection

Janet, sixteen years old, attended a party with her friends. She was young, vibrant, a joy to be with. As the party was winding down she said good-bye to her friends and slid into the back seat of a neighbor's car for the ride home. Tragedy struck. No one had been drinking alcohol, but the driver was speeding. As he approached the curve in the road that led to Janet's house, he lost control of the car. Janet was not wearing a seat belt and was thrown from the car. She was conscious for a brief time after the accident, but when the ambulance arrived she was pronounced dead from internal injuries.

At school the next day Janet's friends gathered, cried, and talked with guidance counselors. A special place was set aside for prayer. Flowers and notes written by her friends were left at Janet's locker. It seemed like everyone who knew Janet attended both her wake and funeral. Tears, hugs, and stories about Janet somehow comforted her friends. Janet's parents and the driver of the car were beside themselves with grief. Students, friends, clergy, and teachers brought food to Janet's house. Some of Janet's friends gathered to pray together.

In time a tennis tournament was established in her honor. Proceeds from the tournament funded a scholarship for a needy child to attend college. Janet's school also established a road race with all proceeds going to the local Girl's Club. Janet's death changed the lives of those who loved her. But by sharing their grief and affirming their faith that through Christ's resurrection this life is a preparation for the next, Janet's family and friends have kept her spirit alive and supported one another in life in the presence of death.

Quiet Time

Response

Pass out pencils and papers with the words, "The Lord is near to the broken-hearted and comforts those who are crushed in spirit."

Leader	Our first response to God's word will be to write on the back of the papers the name or names of a deceased person for whom you would like to pray. You may also write the name of someone you love who has moved away or moved out of your life. Our response to the prayers will be, "The Lord is near to the broken-hearted and comforts those who are crushed in spirit."
Pray-er One	You are a God of life, we now pray for those people we love who have died. *Invite members of the congregation to name people at this time.* May they enjoy lasting life with you, we pray,
All	The Lord is near to the broken-hearted and comforts those who are crushed in spirit.

Pray-er Two	God of love, we pray that the words of Jesus may be fulfilled, "Blessed are they who mourn for they shall be comforted."
All	The Lord is near to the broken-hearted and comforts those who are crushed in spirit.
Pray-er Three	Loving God, you deliver our souls from death. Keep our feet from stumbling, so that we may walk before you in the land of the living. We pray,
All	The Lord is near to the broken-hearted and comforts those who are crushed in spirit.
Pray-er Four	I invite each of you to recite the response silently to yourself. Replace the words "broken-hearted" and "those" with the name of the person or persons which you wrote on your papers.
All	The Lord is near to (*name*) and comforts (*name*), crushed in spirit.

Invite the young people to put their hand gently on the shoulder of the person beside or in front of them.

Leader	God of the grieving, you shall wipe all tears from our eyes; and there shall be no more death, no more sorrow, no more crying, neither shall there be any pain. Bless us now Creator, Savior, and Sanctifier and comfort all those who are crushed in spirit. We ask you to bless us all, and deepen our faith in the resurrection of Jesus, our hope of eternal life.
All	The Lord is near to the broken-hearted and comforts those crushed in spirit. Amen.

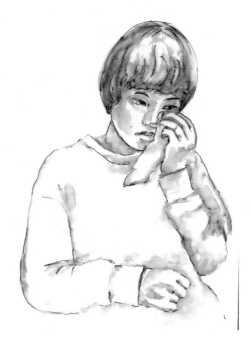

CHAPTER 6

Beautiful People, or People of Lasting Beauty?

Christian Role Models

Times for Use
- All Saints Day
- Feast of St. Peter and Paul
- Presentation on moral values and the culture
- Feast of St. Francis

Introduction

Leader   I caught an unexpected glimpse of American culture through the words of a high school senior. She said, "I don't like the culture of America. I hear children complaining about how little money their parents spend on them. I hear wives complaining about how little money their husbands make when compared to other husbands. I hear husbands complain about how much money their wives cost them. We have everything, but we hate living!"

The happiness promised by those smiling faces in television commercials is not enough for us. The popularity promised to us by wearing the right clothes, driving the right car, and hanging out with the right crowd is too temporary, too limited, too superficial, and too costly. Our need for joy and for love is spiritual. This need cannot be satisfied by what is offered by the media or shopping malls. Where can we search for satisfaction for our longing? Where can we discover lives of substance, lives that stand for something?

We can begin by looking at the lives of our parents, friends, coaches, and members of the clergy. People like Pope John Paul II, Dorothy Day, Dr. Martin Luther King, Jr., and Mother Teresa of Calcutta offer us examples worthy of study and imitation. They did not allow the scintillating distractions offered by the culture of individualism and materialism to capture their minds and hearts. These people are examples of true freedom. They took to heart the words of St. Francis, "Preach the gospel, and sometimes use words."

As we pray, we may ask ourselves some pertinent questions. How free am I in this culture? Do I decide what I will think, how I will act, and what clothes I will wear; or do magazines and television commercials think for me? Am I a person of character and conscience? Do I think for myself and feel my own feelings, or do I constantly look outside myself to discover what I feel and how I should think about things? Who are the people that I choose for role models?

Call to Prayer

Leader Let us remember that we are in the holy presence of a loving God. Loving God, we live in a world where other people tell us how we should dress, what we should think, and how we should spend our leisure time. Help us to learn from those who have resisted that temptation. Show us those people who have developed all their gifts and discovered joy in life by loving you and serving the most needy of your children. We pray through Jesus our Lord and brother,

All Amen.

Scripture

Leader   In the Scripture readings we are reminded not to allow attachment to material possessions to stop us from being able to love completely. Jesus says when we have our priorities straight, we will experience God's love now and be filled with God's presence forever in the life to come.

Reader One   A reading of the gospel according to Luke. (Luke 19:16–30) *Because of the length of this passage, two readers can be used.*

Luke 19:16–26

Reader Two   Luke 19:27–30

Pause

Reflection

Presenter One   Did you see him? Did you hear his challenge? I watched his body move ever so slowly. He shuffled more than he walked. His head remained bent, looking at the ground. He was bowed with age, frail, and his body weak. Yet, when this frail frame of a man spoke, his words flashed truth like lightning illuminating the St. Louis sky. His words were like a fountain inviting all the tired, weary people to drink. I speak, of course, of Pope John Paul II. The Pope had a sparkle in his eye right into his old age, a sparkle that was a window to his soul. Everyone knew what he stood for, even those who disagreed with him.

Presenter Two   I think too of Dorothy Day, co-founder of the Catholic Worker Movement. She used her gift of leadership to open houses of hospitality for the poor, and her gift of writing to inform readers about the nonviolence of Jesus, and about the way the Catholic Church stands with the unemployed and oppressed. Mother Teresa of Calcutta brought Christ's love to the dying and impoverished of India because she saw Jesus in each one. It was Mother Teresa who reminded a governor by phone that in killing a prisoner on death row, he was doing the same to Christ. Martin Luther King, Jr. suffered verbal and physical harassment, attempts on his life, threats to his wife and children, and years spent in jail in order to free blacks from laws that oppressed them. His nonviolent love in the face of oppression freed the white man from the need to hate and persecute black people.

Presenter Three	Pope John Paul II, Dorothy Day, Mother Teresa, Martin Luther King, Jr., and other role models appeal to our hearts about the heart of living. Their message is this: caring for the poor and those in need is our business. They point out that accomplishments that the culture sees as signs of success—college degrees and titles after our names—mean little if these widen the gap between the rich and poor. They become signs that we are forgetting our neighbor's needs. These people remind us that life is not the exclusive right of the wealthy and powerful, but also belongs to the weak, the unborn, the elderly, and those on death row.
	Finally, in a world consumed by the desire for power they declare that peace is not the absence of conflict. Peace is not living in our own private worlds while others suffer outside. But peace is the hard work of establishing justice for all. Pope John Paul, Dorothy Day, Martin Luther King, Jr., and Mother Teresa; everyone knows what they stand for. What about you? What do *you* stand for?

Quiet Time

Response

Leader	In a culture bored by the failure of material goods to produce any lasting satisfaction in life, there are people who encourage us to forget ourselves, to look deep within ourselves and society to discover the passions, values, goals, and activities that will open the door to a purposeful and joyful life. William Faulkner said that there should be in every person something non-negotiable, something for which we stand at all costs. We now pray for the gift of knowing what we stand for and the courage to defend it in all circumstances, at all costs.

Give each person a paper with a circle in the middle and five circles surrounding it. Ask the group to reflect on what they value most in life and write that value in the middle circle. Then name a lesser value and place it in a circle around the center. Invite participants to share their responses with a friend in the assembly. When all have shared their responses, continue.

Leader	Our response to the first four petitions will be, "Disturb us, Lord." Our response to the last three petitions will be, "Holy Spirit, grant us courage."
Pray-er One	God of life, when we are too content with what we have, too focused on ourselves,

All	Disturb us, Lord.
Pray-er Two	When we are so bored with life that we just go through the motions,
All	Disturb us, Lord.
Pray-er Three	When we try so hard to be popular that we are caught up in the latest fashion or fad,
All	Disturb us, Lord.
Pray-er Four	When we take life's gifts for granted, such as the ability to see, to hear, to walk, and to make our own decisions,
All	Disturb us, Lord.

At this point with appropriate music playing, invite the young people to place the papers symbolizing their values on a plate at the front of the assembly. Continue with prayer service.

Pray-er Five	Loving God, we thank you for people in our lives who are passionate about life and motivate and energize each of us. For this we pray,
All	Holy Spirit, grant us courage.
Pray-er Six	Loving God, you teach us what matters in life through the example of people like Pope John Paul, Dorothy Day, Dr. Martin Luther King, Jr., Mother Teresa. Help us to get involved with people who serve the needs of the poor and work for peace and justice in our world.
All	Holy Spirit, grant us courage.

Pray-er Seven	Loving God, give us the wisdom to know what we believe, and grant us the courage to stand up for our beliefs in every situation.
All	Holy Spirit, grant us courage.
Pray-er Eight	Loving God, you give us each new day to refresh us. You give us family and friends, teachers and coaches to guide us.

The leader holds up the papers with the personal values of those gathered written on them.

Leader	We offer to you our values; we hold up those things we cherish most in life. May you guide each of us in choosing good values and in following people who have lived lives of integrity and service for the human family. We pray that the gift of our lives joined to Jesus may renew the face of the earth. Holy Spirit, grant us courage and faith and the ability to do your will.
All	Amen.

CHAPTER 7

When God Is Calling

Finding God's Presence in the People I Love

Times for Use
- Retreat Day on the meaning and purpose of Love
- Valentine's Day
- Feast of St. Peter and St. Paul

Introduction

Leader There is no greater experience than to love and be loved. Jesus has said it is by our love that we are known to be his followers. St. John says, God is love. Whoever lives in love lives in God and God lives in that person. Falling in love and staying in love are the repeated themes of song, stage and cinema. This prayer service invites us to reflect on Christ's love for us. It celebrates the presence of God, Christ's love for us in the people we love and those who love us each day. *You may want to make a copy of the following prayer by Fr. Pedro Arupe, S.J., for all present.*

Nothing is more practical than finding God, than falling in love in quite an absolute, final way. What you are in love with, what seizes your imagination, will affect everything. It will decide what will get you out of bed in the morning, what you do with your evenings, how you spend your weekends, what you read, who you know, what breaks your heart, and what amazes you with joy and gratitude. Fall in love, stay in love, and it will decide everything.

To prepare for the prayer service ask participants to write an answer to the questions: What is love? How do I know I am in love? Share some of the responses with the whole group. Next, invite the congregation to look up passages in Scripture that describe the nature and meaning of love. These may be shared among the groups. Some descriptions of love that the group believes are the best may be written on poster board or newsprint. Place a number in the lower corner of each poster to determine the order in which the posters will be brought forward later in the service. This exercise allows the leader to distinguish between different types of love.

In the Greek language three different words distinguish three different types of love. *Eros* is understood as sexual love, *filia* as sister or brotherly love, and *agape* as God's unconditional love for us. Suggested passages are: Matthew 5:1–12, 43–48; Mark 12:28–34; John 13:1–12, 34–35; John 15:9–17; Acts of the Apostles 4:32–35; 1 Corinthians 13:1–13; Colossians 3:12–17; 1 John 4:1–16.

Call to Prayer

Leader   Let us remember we are in the holy presence of a loving God.

All   Amen.

Scripture Reading

Leader   The word passion means to be full of life. When we are truly in love we become passionate people. Our love will be the determining factor in the kind of life we choose to live. In the gospel reading, we see how Mary Magdalene's love for Christ filled her with life and brought her to the tomb early in the morning on the third day after the crucifixion.

Reader   A reading from the gospel according to John. (John 20:1–3, 11–18)

Reflection

Isn't it amazing? When we least expect it we uncover a card, a poem, a picture, or a prayer given to us by someone who is no longer with us. I recently discovered a card entitled, "A Nurses Prayer," which belonged to my mother. Here's what it said:

As I care for my patients today,
Be there with me, O Lord, I pray.
Make my words kind; it means so much.

And in my hands place your healing touch.
Let Your love shine through all that I do,
So those in need may hear and feel you.

This prayer reflects my mother's great love for nursing. Through it she met Christ in the people she served, and they certainly met the love of Christ in her. This is similar to Mary Magdalene in the gospel reading. She loved the Lord, and that love determined how she lived her life. Her life became centered around the person she loved. So it is with each of us. We need to pay attention to who or what we love and realize this is one of the primary ways that God works in our lives. What we love will influence us in a total way. Through our loves we will discover God, and that will determine everything.

Quiet Time

Response

Select some participants to tape their descriptions of love to a room divider or a wall for all to see. Ask them to read the description of love on their poster.

Leader	I invite those people with the newsprint (or poster board) to come forward in order of the number posted on the bottom left corner of the newsprint.
	We now pray to the God of all creation, the Son who is risen, and Holy Spirit who dwells in our hearts, that we may meet God in the people we love and those who love us. Our response will be, "God of love, lead us to live passionately, and discover your holy presence in all those we love."
Presenter One	(Reads from newsprint.)
All	God of love, lead us to live passionately, and discover your holy presence in all those we love.
Presenter Two	(Reads from newsprint.)
All	God of love, lead us to live passionately, and discover your holy presence in all those we love.

After each presenter reads, the response is repeated. When all have come forward, the leader prays.

Leader	Today we celebrate the presence of love in our lives. We thank God that we are made for love. We pray for strong, healthy relationships. We pray in faith that each of us may meet Christ in the loves that shape us each day.

All	God of love, lead us to live passionately, and discover your holy presence in all those we love.
Leader	Please come forward to receive a card with a reminder of love's power to bring God into our lives. *Distribute the cards with the prayer of Fr. Pedro Arupe. S.J., from the Introduction.* Now, let us all read together the reflection by Fr. Arupe.
All	Amen.

CHAPTER 8

Prayer

Our Lifeline to God

Times for Use
- A confirmation retreat
- A presentation on the meaning of prayer
- A class on prayer
- Feast of St. Theresa of Avila or St. John of the Cross

Introduction

Leader

Today we will focus our attention on the experience of prayer. Some people think that prayer is an activity reserved for a specialist in prayer or for "holy" people. The opposite is closer to what is true. Author James Carroll writes: "Prayer is not a special activity reserved for elites of any kind. Prayer is a result of God's presence in human beings." Prayer has been described as raising our minds and hearts to God or as conversation with God. Prayer has been likened to the look between two lovers.

All real prayer is an expression of our faith in God's presence to us. Even our anger at God or our experiences of abandonment and disbelief affirm on another level that we are not God. God's holy presence is both beyond us and at the same time the burning center, the invisible core of our being. This center within each of us invites us into dialogue with God and leads us into God's great mystery which is the fiber and fabric of the world in which we live.

Call to Prayer

Leader Let us remember that we are in the holy presence of our loving God. Loving God, you reveal yourself to us in Scripture. Jesus calls you Abba, loving Father. On the feast of Pentecost you make yourself known as a Holy Spirit of wisdom and compassion. You are also present in us, for we are created in your image and likeness.

The order we discover in our world speaks of your holy presence drawing us to yourself through its beauty. We ask that through faith we may know you in the many ways you reveal yourself to us. May your Holy Spirit be a light to guide us on our journey that all of our searching and longing may lead us to you. We ask this in the name of Jesus, and united in your Holy Spirit.

All Amen.

Scripture Reading

Leader Jesus teaches us that prayer is not to be showy or involve a lot of words. Prayer is to be simple and from the heart. In the Our Father Jesus shares with us his own relationship with God, the intimate bond he shared with his Abba. Before we pray, we spend a moment in silence to become aware of who it is that we are about to address. We know that God loves us as God loves Jesus. With this certainty we pray.

Reader A reading of the gospel according to Matthew. (Matthew 6:6–14)

Reflection

Rabbi Abraham Joshua Heschel tells the story of a shoemaker, who needed advice about his morning prayer. The shoemaker was very good at his trade, and he was also a devout man who prayed daily. The shoemaker would pick up his customer's shoes in the evening, work on them through the evening and early morning, then deliver them to their owners before they left for work. And so the shoemaker asked the rabbi, should he pray before his morning work or should he let the appointed time go by and every once in a while stop working and utter with a sigh: "Woe is me, I haven't prayed yet"? The rabbi replied that, in the sight of the Almighty, perhaps that sigh was worth more than the prayer itself.

Prayer is an attempt to turn our attention toward God. In this regards, both the gospel and the story point to a simple truth. It is the honesty of our prayer, the longing and desire for God, that gets God's attention every time. We look in God's direction and wait. We do this when asking for something, when thanking God for a favor received, when we are angry or sad, or when we sit quietly with God in the silence. We have two ears and one mouth. This fact directs us to do twice as much listening as speaking in prayer.

Sometimes we may be confused about what is the best way to pray, the best method. There are as many ways to pray as there are people. The eucharistic liturgy is the official public prayer of the Church by which Jesus is present in a unique manner. All prayer springs from this and returns to Christ present in the eucharistic celebration. We can use formal prayers like the Our Father and Hail Mary. We can pray from a verse in Scripture, by singing or listening to music, or through dance. We can pray the rosary, or we can pray by watching a sunset. The key in all prayer is our faith in God, our love and trust, the placing of our lives in God's hands. Prayer is the way we keep in touch with God.

Quiet Time

Response

Pass out pencils and paper. Put copies of formal prayers on the tables around the room. Copies of the Our Father, Act of Contrition, Mysteries of the Rosary may be placed strategically around the room. You may choose to use one of these prayers to get ideas for your prayer. Other prayerful reflections may be provided.

Leader	Let's spend a few minutes forming a prayer we want to offer to God. Think about what you want to say to God. Is it a statement, a question, a poem, something uniquely yours, or the lyrics to a song? When you are ready write your prayer on the paper provided. Create some symbol or visual image to accompany your prayer. Remember, you don't have to write a perfect prayer only your prayer. Let it be a true expression of you and your faith in God's love for you. *Allow time for completion of the task. When all have finished, the prayer follows.*
	We know we are in the holy presence of God. We invite members of the community to share their prayers as a way to respond to God. Our response will be, "Loving God, hear our prayer."
Pray-er One	*Read prayer.*
Response	Loving God, hear our prayer.
Pray-er Two	*Read prayer.*

Response	Loving God, hear our prayer.
Leader	Jesus, you taught your followers the art of prayer. Today, you pray with us through the Holy Spirit. We thank you for this marvelous means of communication with you. Increase our faith in your holy presence and lead us to pray at all times and in all places. We offer our prayer in union with Jesus and we pray by the power of your Holy Spirit.
All	Amen.

Participants may be invited to keep their prayers as the first offering of a prayer journal to which they can add prayers as they choose.

CHAPTER 9

God of Beautiful Things

Embracing God in the Midst of Cruelty

Times for Use
- Before graduation
- Confirmation preparation
- Feast of St. Francis
- Before summer vacation

Introduction

Leader

Events like graduation, receiving the sacraments, and weddings are a source of joy for many people. There is joy in the smiles of the graduates, the hugs from family and friends, and the exchange of vows between bride and groom. The joy and beauty of such events is challenged daily by the headlines in bold black print across the front page of newspapers. War, famine, homelessness, and unemployment may convince us that the entire world is wrapped in pain. At such times we wonder whether or not God wants us to enjoy life's simple blessings. But as Trappist nun Sr. Miriam Pollard reminds us, "Even our cruelty to one another can not send into exile the God of beautiful things."

We pray for the gift to see both the joy and the pain in the light of faith and in the gospel of Jesus Christ. We do not need to seek the beautiful while fleeing the painful. Rather, we need to see in both the mystery of God's providence for each of us. We respond to new people and to new events with trust in God's presence in every moment of every day.

Call to Prayer

Leader	God of beautiful things, your presence touches everything that is full of color, shape, and order.
Pray-er One	You transform winter into spring, caterpillars into butterflies, barren trees into green-leafed maples.
Pray-er Two	You care for us through community, through sacrament, through the order of nature and the quiet of solitude.
Pray-er Three	When fear grips our minds and we feel alone and isolated, help us to know you are present in the quiet of an empty church, in the unchanging cycle of the setting of the sun, in your holy presence in the sacrament of the Eucharist, and in the community you have placed nearest to us.
All	Lead us to recognize your healing presence through the many ways you are there for us. We pray this in Christ's name and in union with your Holy Spirit, who dwells in our hearts.
All	Amen.

Scripture Reading

Leader	The story of Thomas doubting the presence of Jesus after the resurrection is our story too. The death of Jesus on the cross in all its cruel and brutal concreteness blocked sight of the presence of beautiful, joyful things. Like Thomas, we too need the power of God's grace to help us to take off our blindfolds and see God at work in our world.
Reader	A reading from the gospel according to John. (John 24:24–29)

Reflection

There is a legend that tells the story of an old monk and a crown of thorns. One Good Friday, the monk made a crown of thorns, like the one placed on the head of Jesus before the crucifixion, and placed it on the altar of the nearby church. The crown was to remind all who viewed it of the affliction Jesus suffered during his passion and death, and of the cruelty of his tormentors.

On Easter Sunday, the monk ran to the church to remove the crown of thorns from its resting place. When he opened the door to the church, he was amazed! A beautiful fragrance filled his senses. He followed the sun's rays through the stained-glass window to the place where the crown had been. The twisted thorns had been changed into a beautiful bouquet of roses. They bathed the monk's eyes in the softest beauty and filled the church with an exhilarating fragrance. The symbol of death, pain, and hopelessness had become a life-giving sign of healing and hope.

Both the gospel story and the monk's tale remind us that we are created for joy. Undoubtedly, we will face suffering and pain in which we see no meaning. Yet, if we seek to discover God's presence in the pain, we will find it in faith, prayer, and the support of community. Thomas learned that death can be transformed into the door to everlasting life. The monk learned that God would transform even the most severe affliction into joy. We pray for the gift of faith found in the promises of Christ, and for a faith-filled community to support us.

Quiet Time

Response

The response will include writing and choral prayer. The young people will be invited to write the name of a person who is suffering and for whom they would like to pray. They could also choose some painful experience in which they would like to see meaning. Ask the teens to hold these papers as the prayer service begins.

Leader	God of all life, sometimes we are afraid to experience joy because of the suffering and pain in our world. Sometimes we try to escape pain by using dangerous and harmful methods. We now pray that we discover your will in all the events in our lives. We look to our faith community to support us during times of crisis. We pray this in faith, with hope, and united in love.
All	Amen.
Pray-er One	Together, we express our desire to see grief and sorrow in the light of God's uninterrupted love for us.
Left side	When grief and sorrow overcome us and we doubt in your holy presence, we pray,
Right side	Lord, we believe. Help our unbelief.
Right side	When our lives seem to be all thorns and no roses, we pray,

Left side	Lord, we believe. Help our unbelief.
Left side	When our friends look to us for support in their time of sorrow, we pray,
Right side	Lord, we believe. Help our unbelief.
Right side	When loneliness is our only companion, we pray,
Left side	Lord, we believe. Help our unbelief.
Left side	For the gift of our bodies, minds, and imagination, we pray,
Right side	My soul magnifies the Lord, my spirit rejoices in God my savior.
Right side	For the gift of friends and people who bring love into our lives, we pray,
Left side	My soul magnifies the Lord, my spirit rejoices in God my savior.
Left side	For the beauty of the natural world and the smile on the face of our friends, we pray,
Right side	My soul magnifies the Lord, my spirit rejoices in God my savior.
Right side	For the gift of our families, we pray,
Left side	My soul magnifies the Lord, my spirit rejoices in God my savior.

While music plays, invite to place the names of the people for whom they prayed on the altar. When all have completed this, the leader continues.

Leader	God of healing, we believe that your love surrounds us during moments of sorrow and moments of joy. Teach us to view all that is beautiful with gratitude as your sign that we are created for joy. Lead us to penetrate the mystery of suffering with the light of faith. Help us to look to prayer, to the Christian community, and to Scripture to uncover your presence in our lives. May the Holy Spirit lead us to the conviction that even our suffering can become an occasion for new life with you, and a means to ultimate joy. We pray with faith in your holy presence with us now.
All	Amen.

CHAPTER 10

A New Beginning

The Healing Power of Forgiveness

Times for Use
- Preparation the sacrament of Reconciliation
- Holy Week
- Presentation on making relationships last

Introduction

Leader

A song once declared, "You always hurt the ones you love." At times, all of us hurt the one's we love. I'm sure you have experienced this in your lives. Our relationships are a mixture of kindness and, at times, selfishness. What is true of individuals is also true of groups. There are fractures in relationships that last for years, even resulting in war and oppression.

Jesus asks each of us to heal broken relationships with forgiveness. Without forgiveness, relationships are doomed to failure. Forgiveness is the healing ointment that cleans and mends the old wounds. We are to forgive just as Jesus has forgiven each of us. The proverb says, "In every pardon there is love." Jesus forgives us so that we may bear his forgiveness to those in our world who need it most. We may ask, is forgiveness important in my life? Do I celebrate the sacrament of reconciliation to experience its healing and comfort? Are there people I refuse to forgive? Are there people from whom I refuse to seek forgiveness?

Call to Prayer

Leader Let us remember we are in the holy presence of a loving God. God of mercy, Jesus walked among us as a reconciler, one who forgave and healed relationships broken by selfishness and sin. Jesus knows forgiveness can transform lives. He wills us to experience his forgiveness and he invites us to share this healing force with those we have harmed or those who have harmed us. Because we have been forgiven and healed by Christ, help us to allow his forgiveness to flow to others through us. We pray this in his name and by the power of the Holy Spirit who dwells in our hearts.

All Amen.

Scripture Reading

Leader The reading proclaims forgiveness is central to the life of the Christian. Let's listen carefully to the beautiful description of the qualities that characterize our lives as followers of Christ.

Reader A reading from the letter of St. Paul to the Colossians. (Colossians 3:12–15)

Pause

Reflection

Sometimes something happens in our lives that allow us to see ourselves in a new way, to see ourselves through the eyes of another. This happened to me one Thanksgiving Day. Our parish invited members of the Narragansett Indian tribe to speak at our prayer service. On Thanksgiving morning our pastoral minister told us that they had declined our invitation. They could not celebrate with us because it was for them a reminder of all they had lost by aiding the white settlers. This included their land, lives, and culture. Thanksgiving was for them a day of mourning and sorrow.

As Thanksgiving is time when we share gratitude for the earth and for our sisters and brothers we wanted to show our concern for the members of the tribe. Perhaps, if we continued contact with the members of the tribe, they would come to visit with us on another occasion. The attempt to invite back into our lives and into our families those who feel rejected is a practice Jesus embraced in his life. Forgiveness as an attitude and an action is at the heart of the life and ministry of Jesus. Let us reflect on our attitudes and actions to determine where and why forgiveness is neglected by us as a way to heal broken relationships.

Quiet Time

Response

Place small wooden crosses on the altar or table for each participant in the service. If the sacrament of reconciliation is to be celebrated, this is the time for an examination of conscience and the following prayers will conclude the service. A card with an examination of conscience and appropriate readings can be left in the pews or on the chairs. If the sacrament is not being celebrated, continue with the service.

Leader	Let us now stand to pray that we may become ambassadors of God's forgiveness in our homes, schools, and other communities. Our response will be, "Forgive us our sins as we forgive those who harm us."
Pray-er One	God of mercy, Jesus came among us to offer us your forgiveness for our sins and to send us out as bearers of forgiveness to others. We thank you for the sacrament of reconciliation. Because you forgive us our sins, may we bring forgiveness to those who ask it from us. For this we pray,
All	Forgive us our sins as we forgive those who harm us.
Pray-er Two	God of mercy, Jesus said we are to forgive as often as people ask it of us. Help us to forgive especially when it is difficult. Protect us from the prison that revenge and holding grudges can build around us. Help us to realize how such attitudes poison our ability to act freely with others. For this we pray,
All	Forgive us our sins as we forgive those who harm us.
Pray-er Three	God of mercy, forgiveness is a way of welcoming people back into our lives. Make us big hearted enough to encourage those who are separated from us to return to give our relationship one more chance. For this we pray,
All	Forgive us our sins as we forgive those who harm us.
Pray-er Four	God of mercy, we are the people given new life to love through the forgiveness you offer to us each day. May your Holy Spirit fill each of us with the spirit of forgiveness and gratitude. May your spirit be like a light to guide us in our relationships each day. For this we pray,

All	Forgive us our sins as we forgive those who harm us.
Leader	Jesus showed the extent of God's forgiveness by his death and resurrection. His words of forgiveness for his executioners, "Father forgive them they don't know what they are doing," is a cry reaching over the centuries imploring us to forgive as he did.
	At this time I invite each person to come forward to receive a small cross as a reminder of the power and cost of God's forgiveness. Wearing the cross is also a sign that we too will make forgiveness central in our lives. Those handing out the crosses may say, "Receive this sign of God's mercy." *Those receiving the crosses may say, "Amen." When all have come forward, the kiss of peace can be shared. End the service with the Our Father.*

CHAPTER 11

I'll Hold My Own Hand

To Be Oneself with Others

> **Times for Use**
> - The beginning of a new year of school or catechetical instruction
> - Retreat presentation on the art of being unique while being with others
> - Retreat presentation on identity and personal integrity
> - All Saints Day

Introduction

Leader

Each of us experiences times when we are not sure whether it is appropriate to seek the help of others. Sometimes, out of a false sense of independence, we try to go it alone when we really need help. Some examples, the need to grieve the loss of a friend, trying to decide whether to become sexually active, or deciding what to do after high school. At other times we may seek help from others when we really should go it alone. Some common examples include, copying homework, asking a friend to lie about where we were after curfew, asking our parents to get us free from a traffic violation, or asking the teacher for the answer to a question that we can discover through our own research.

Thomas Merton once wrote, "We are called to share with God the work of creating the truth of our own identity." As we begin our prayer service, you may want to reflect on these words. The new millennium presents new challenges that demand common effort. Above all the tasks ahead invite participation of people who know they are on a spiritual journey to uncover their identity hidden in the Mystery of God. You may also ask yourself, What makes me the unique person I am? Do I believe I am creating my identity with God through the decisions I make? Am I a person who can stand on my own when appropriate and just as easily ask others for help when the need arises?

Please note that the activity in the Response section may be used here in the beginning of the prayer service.

Call to Prayer

Leader

Let us remember we are in the holy presence of a loving God. Jesus, our brother, you experienced the challenge of being yourself. You discovered in your relationships people with whom you could share your hopes and fears. Your time alone in prayer taught you how to be yourself and affirm your values even when others rejected you for standing by your conscience. We pray that in your loving presence we may draw closer to you. Help us to learn how to be ourselves at all times while being a good friend, loving daughter or son, and thoughtful member of our school community. Teach us to value our integrity more than we seek the approval of others. We offer this prayer guided by the Holy Spirit who lives in our hearts.

All

Amen.

Scripture Reading

Leader

Our identity is not given to us but something we form each day through our decisions. As we try to discover who we are, we sometimes do things that are misunderstood by those around us. Let's listen to an account of a time when Jesus' parents didn't understand his attempt to stand on his own two feet when discussing religious matters with the elders of Judaism. Notice too how Jesus trusted the guidance of his parents when they directed him to follow them home.

Reader

A reading of the gospel according to Luke. (Luke 2:41–52)

Pause

Reflection

On a recent visit, my daughter-in-law, Wendy, shared the following story. She was taking my two-and-a-half-year-old grandson, Aidan, for a walk. As they approached a busy intersection Wendy lowered her hand toward Aidan and said, "Aidan, hold mommy's hand while we cross the street." Without hesitating Aidan looked up at his mother and responded, "I'll hold my own hand, Mommy." With this he folded one of his hands into the other.

Both the gospel and the story of Aidan's independence offer examples of the difficulty in growing up. When do we go it alone, and when is it the wise decision to reach out to others for help? When do we trust in our own powers and gifts, and when to learn from the guidance and wisdom of others? Each of us could ask ourselves, are we free to ask for help when we need it or are we too proud or fearful to seek the advice of others? On the other hand, some of us may be overly dependent on others and fail to accept the challenges necessary for our growth into mature Christian adults. Gracefully learning when to be independent and when to ask others for help leads us to create with God our unique self.

Quiet Time

Response

Situations where a decision must be made can either be projected on a screen or put on newsprint in front of the assembly. Some possibilities are: choosing a college, deciding whether or not to drink at a party where alcohol is available, deciding what to do about an unplanned pregnancy, deciding whether to go on vacation for spring break or to work in Appalachia for Habitat for Humanity, whether or not to keep the answers to an important test that you accidentally found.

As each situation is read, invite each participant to decide whether he or she would seek help with the decision or try it alone. Ask them to move to one side of the room if they would go it alone and to another side of the room if they would seek help. Ask for volunteers to explain their choices. After some explanations have been shared, have a brief discussion, creating a list of five guiding principles to help young people to know when to seek help. When you finish this activity, continue with the prayer service.

Leader   Let us join together in prayer. We seek God's guidance in those decisions that will take us from adolescence to adulthood. We now pray for each other that we may know the satisfaction of being independent and standing on our own two feet. We pray also that each of us may have the humility to seek the help of others in time of need. The response will be, "Loving God, you hold each of us in the palm of your hand."

Pray-er One	Jesus, you were once a young person like us. We ask you to help us make decisions that will help us be true to ourselves and avoid actions that we would be ashamed of. For this we pray,
All	Loving God, you hold us in the palm of your hand.
Pray-er Two	Jesus, you too know how lonely life can be at times. Help us go to you when we are lonely; help us share our loneliness with friends and adults who love us. For this we pray,
All	Loving God, you hold us in the palm of your hand.
Pray-er Three	Jesus, you grew into a person of wisdom and compassion. Support us when we stumble in trying to be our best selves. Help us see that we are not a finished product, but on our way to our own adulthood. Lead us to the awareness that if we stay true to you and to our own conscience, what seems impossible today will be accomplished tomorrow. For this we pray,
All	Loving God, you hold us in the palm of your hand.
Pray-er Four	God of all change, we thank you for creating each of us as unique and gifted human beings. Guide us to help one another discover the great gift we are in your eyes. Help us share our gifts generously with others each day. We pray this in the name of Jesus, our Lord and brother.

All	Loving God, you hold us in the palm of your hand.

Ask participants to raise their right hand in blessing over the person in front of them. Initiate the following prayer.

Leader	You are a God of love. You care for us as a loving parent, even when we feel far from you.
Pray-er Five	We offer to you our hopes and fears about growing into adulthood. Work with us, please, to create our unique identities.
All	You hold us in the palm of your hand.
Leader	We thank you for your faithful love and ask that we may be open to your presence and care in our lives.
All	You hold us in the palm of your hands.
Leader	Bless us, O God, Creator, Redeemer, and Sanctifier, now and forever,
All	Amen.

CHAPTER 12

Will You Be There for Me?

The Importance of Friends

> **Times for use**
> - Beginning of a new school year
> - Welcome for new members in religious ed classes
> - Prayer service before a dance or prom
> - Confirmation theme: Jesus, my friend

Introduction

Leader   Friendship is one of the most precious and lasting gifts that God has shared with us. The successes of the new millennium will demand the support of intimate friendships. The presence of good friends can encourage us to be honest, respectful, and kind. It has been said that in seeking friends we are seeking God. Habib Sahabib writes, "Blessed is he who hungers for friends—for though he may not realize it, his soul is crying out for God." As we begin our prayer service you may ask yourself, what is friendship? Why is it necessary? What qualities make a good friend? Can the desire to please friends at times lead me to betray my deepest values? In what ways to friends influence to person I am becoming each day?

53

Call to Prayer

Leader	Let us pause to remember that we are in the presence of a loving God.
Pray-er One	God, protector of friendships, you are the Holy Trinity, the God who is, the Jesus who is risen and the Spirit who dwells in our hearts. You are a relationship of love.
Pray-er Two	When we seek to love and to be loved by our friends, we share in your love. We thank you for this great gift that fills us with such joy and affection. Teach us how to seek goodness in our friends and to choose friends wisely. Help us to be a good influence on our friends.
Pray-er Three	Holy Spirit, fill our friendships with respect for each other. Above all, may we learn that it is you who loves us in the love of our friends. We pray this in the name of Jesus and by the power of the Holy Spirit who dwells in our hearts.
All	Amen.

Scripture Reading

Leader	Friends are what turn an ordinary day into a new adventure. We look forward to seeing our friends, to sharing their stories, to listening to their problems, and sharing in their joy. Friends teach us the importance of trust and respect. They show us how to be close but not smothering, how to balance companionship with the need for independence. Friends invite us to be our true selves in their presence. They help us to discover those qualities that become part of our identity, the unique gift that we offer the world each day. In the Scripture reading we see friends and friendship through the eyes of Jesus.
Reader	A reading from the gospel according to John. (John 15:12–15)

Pause

Reflection

Two options for reflection on the following story are provided.

Perhaps you know this story told to me by a friend. Once a young woman had a facial tumor that had to be removed. The doctor told her and her husband that the surgery might cause nerve damage to the face. He couldn't be sure. When the operation was over, the tumor had been successfully removed but the woman's face was distorted due to damage to nerves controlling facial muscles. When the doctor told the woman, she was both grateful for the removal of the tumor and saddened by the damage done to her facial nerves. Naturally she wondered how her husband would respond to her disfigured face. Her husband standing in the corner of the room looked lovingly at his wife. He then walked slowly to her bed, leaned forward and while reshaping his lips to match her own, he kissed her gently and lovingly. The doctor watched in amazement. He later told a friend that he believed he had witnessed the holy presence of God in that hospital room on that day in the kiss of the man for his wife.

Reflection One

The act of love in this story uncovers for us some of the central qualities of friendship described by Jesus in John's gospel. Jesus says we are his friends because he has revealed to us all that is in God's heart for us. Friends share what is most intimate to them. The friendship of the couple in the story is evident in the willingness of the wife to allow her husband to be there for her surgery and to witness its effects. The knowledge the husband gains about his wife, the awareness of her facial deformity, could have had lasting negative affects on their relationship. But his love put her need before his own and he kissed her in such a way that his lips took the shape of hers; he identified with her. This is a kind of giving your life for another that Jesus says is a sign of a true friend. Empathy, putting ourselves in the place of another, is a sign of true friendship.

Reflection Two

The love of the husband for his wife and she for him is a consequence of the couple's free consent to love each other. Their mutual respect and their trust nourish their love. Free consent, respect, and trust are the basis of real friendship, too. Free consent means there is no pressure to make a choice one way or the other. Mutual respect means the two people are equal in the relationship; one is not superior to the other. Each remains free to hold his or her opinions and feelings in the relationship. Finally, friendship is not all give or take by one person in the relationship. Rather, trust leads to reciprocity, a mutual exchange of gifts one from the other. As in all friendships, independence, love, and joy enrich both parties in the relationship. The result is both parties feel independence and love, joy and freedom.

When we consider friendship in our lives, it is helpful to keep in touch with stories that illustrate the great gift and great responsibility that is part of being a friend.

Response

Place four lighted candles on the table or altar with a large candle in the middle.

Leader	Our response will be, "Lord Jesus, bless our friends. Keep them healthy and safe." The light of the candle reminds us of the light of Christ's love present in each of our friendships.
	Let us pray. Jesus, you call us your friends. We turn to you in prayer to express gratitude for our friends. We ask you to bless in us the gifts needed to support true and lasting friendships.
All	Lord Jesus, bless our friends. Keep them healthy and safe.
Pray-er One	Jesus, through your friends, Martha, Mary, and Lazarus, you found comfort in times of sorrow and support for the work in your ministry. Our friends comfort us too, and we look to them for support in our daily lives. With glad hearts we pray to you.
All	Lord Jesus, bless our friends. Keep them healthy and safe.
Pray-er Two	Jesus, our friendships are based on mutual respect and the free consent to be friends. Help us, Lord, to develop a deep sense of respect for others and teach us to honor the gift of free choice in all of our relationships. With glad hearts we pray to you.
All	Lord Jesus, bless our friends. Keep them healthy and safe.

Invite each person one at a time to take a lit candle from the altar and name a friend for whom they are grateful or a friend who is in need of the community's prayers. For example, "For my friend Mary, let us pray." After each name is mentioned the person naming returns to his or her place and the congregation responds, "For the gift of Mary's friendship and for her intentions, we pray to the Lord." When finished, conclude the ceremony.

Pray-er Three	Loving God, Jesus numbers us as his friends. In the love of our friends we encounter your love for us. We are grateful for a gift, which has such a profound influence on our lives. Teach us to be good friends and to look upon our friends as a priceless treasure. With glad hearts we pray to the God of friendship.
All	For the gift of friendship we thank you, Lord. Amen.

Candles are extinguished. Participants may keep their candle as reminders of the light of Christ's love in each friendship.

CHAPTER 13

Holiness and Wholeness

Sexual Maturity

Times for Use
- Confirmation retreat on holiness
- After a discussion on dating relationships
- Before dances or proms
- Celebration of the gift of sexuality
- Christmas

Introduction

Leader

One of the greatest challenges facing young people today is to develop into sexually mature women and men. Messages from the media often separate sex from love, pleasure from commitment, and the sex drive from mature sexuality. This places great barriers in the way of the self-knowledge necessary for sexual maturity to develop. Sexuality is first of all about personal identity and personhood before it is about relationships. Sexuality is who I am before it becomes something I share.

One girl who was a senior in high school told me, "Teenagers want to feel loved so they have sex. They want another to fill an empty spot within themselves." The poet Rainer Maria Rilke offers us wise advice when he suggests that we are to become a world unto ourselves for the sake of another. That is the real work of the adolescent years. It is a time to develop all our gifts, to get to know our world and ourselves. We are to become as complete a person as possible.

If we are to become mature sexually, certain questions present themselves. Is sexuality something I do or is it the person I am? Why is it so easy to confuse sex with love? How can I become a sexually mature person? What does Jesus becoming one of us have to do with my sexuality?

Call to Prayer

Leader   Let us remember we are in the holy presence of a loving God. Loving God, by becoming one of us Jesus joined our humanity to your divinity. We are one in body, mind, emotions, and imagination. We are one person with many parts. Help us to understand how wondrously we are made.

Teach us to direct our bodies and our physical desires to the good of the whole person. Teach us to distinguish sex from love. Help us, loving God, to know our values so our relationships may be built on honesty, trust, and respect. May we praise you, our creator, through the respectful use of our minds, bodies, and emotions. We pray this in union with Jesus and by the power of the Holy Spirit who dwells in our hearts.

All   Amen.

Scripture

Leader   We live in a world that separates our sex drive from love and encourages us to act on our instincts without thought of the consequences. The painful results of such behavior are all too prevalent in the society around us. But how are we to grow up and become the kind of woman or man that we want to become? How can knowledge and love guide us into sexual maturity? St. Paul points to the Christian response.

Reader   A reading from the letter of Paul to the Corinthians. (1 Corinthians 6:12–14)

Pause

Reflection

I remember vividly a sophomore in high school whom I met a number of years ago. She was bright, pretty, and athletic. So I was amazed when one day she came to my office in tears. I invited her to sit and waited for some of the tears to stop. I then asked her what was the problem. She responded, "I am never going to trust anyone again as long as I live." I wanted to remind her that if she could not trust, then she would never have a loving, fulfilling relationship of any kind. Instead, I said nothing and listened to her tell how she thought her boyfriend, a senior, loved her. They had shared sexual intercourse and then he broke up with her. She was emotionally drained and felt betrayed to the core of her being.

Although she was not pregnant nor did she have a venereal disease, this girl was deeply wounded. Was the young man who used her for momentary excitement going to heal the hole in her soul for which he was in great part responsible? Would she ever learn to trust again? What would happen to her if she didn't learn to trust?

Adolescence is a time to learn about yourself and to become your own best friend. It is a time to learn about the world. It is a time to develop your gifts, to get to know others, and to experience the many ways outside of sex to share and receive affection. It is a time to become all one can be in order to have something to give to a lasting relationship when the right time comes along. It is a time to learn how to glorify the Lord with our bodies.

Have pictures of athletes, artists, scientists, factory workers, secretaries, etc., posted around the room. Either select young people beforehand or invite volunteers to go to one picture and explain how the person photographed is serving others and therefore praising God. Be sure to have pictures of families and people sharing signs of affection. When some of the pictures have been explained continue.

Leader   We are reminded by our Scripture reading and by the pictures that we have just viewed together that we can use our bodies to develop our talents and to serve our neighbors near and far. When our bodies serve others in love they fulfill the purpose for which they were created.

Quiet Time

Response

Leader   Our sexuality is the mystery of our being one in body, mind, emotions and imagination. With our physical bodies we can either do great harm to another or we can use them to love and to serve others. When we love, we glorify God with our bodies. We will now pray together to ask God to help us to know who we are as sexual people and to thank God for the gift of our sexuality. Our response is, "Only we can glorify God with our bodies."

Prayers of Intercession

Pray-er One	God created us as sexual people; we are created in the image and likeness of God.
All	Only we can glorify God with our bodies.
Pray-er Two	God created the sex drive, our minds, our wills, our imaginations, and emotions. Our bodies are at the service of our whole person.
All	Only we can glorify God with our bodies.
Pray-er Three	God gave us the gift of free will; only we know whether our words are truthful and which of our actions will harm or help another.
All	Only we can glorify God with our bodies.
Pray-er Four	God created in us the power to love; only we know our motives. We alone know whether we are acting out of love or acting selfishly.
All	Only we can glorify God with our bodies.
Leader	Loving God, you created us for joy. We know that joy results from doing your will and from using your gifts properly. We pray in gratitude for the great gift of human sexuality. Help us to know ourselves, to develop our gifts and to become people who have something worthwhile to share when we are ready for the lasting gift that sexual intimacy demands. We pray this in gratitude to God our creator, to Jesus our redeemer, and to the Holy Spirit who dwells in our hearts.
All	Amen.

CHAPTER 14

In God's Own Image

Overcoming Stereotypes

Times for Use
- All Saints Day
- Presentation on the theme of overcoming stereotypes
- Theme of loving our neighbor

Introduction

Leader

There is an old Yoruba proverb that says, "The river that forgets its own source will dry up." This applies to us as we try to love others as Jesus invites us to love. Our attempts to love others are sometimes frustrated by our own secret or hidden prejudices. God's great love for us as made known in Jesus is the source of our love as Christian young people. If we hate or have biased views of certain people or groups of people, these come from a source other than Jesus. As the proverb states, if we forget the source of our love, it will dry up. We will now pray that we will keep alive that love in us that is from God. We pray too for the grace to face and overcome the destructive force of prejudice in our lives.

To help the young people to focus on the theme, invite a brief examination of conscience on their experience of discrimination and prejudice. After a brief reflection ask them to pair up with one other person and each take one minute to share while the other listens. Next, ask them to invite two additional people into the group. The process is repeated. After the second sharing, ask a spokesperson for each group or a selection of groups to share one or two of the experiences shared. Invite those gathered to bring the people mentioned into their prayer.

Call to Prayer

Leader   Let us remember we are in the holy presence of a loving God. Spirit of Truth, we pray for the ability to see the world around us clearly. Make us alert to the many types of people with whom we live. Awaken us to the opportunities to meet people who are different from us and protect us from prejudices that would blind us to the unique gift of every person. Teach us to love our neighbor as an expression of our love for you. We pray this in union with Jesus our Lord and brother.

All   Amen.

Scripture Reading

Leader   Jesus presented a challenge for his Jewish neighbors. He ate with sinners and outcasts. When he told the parable of the Good Samaritan, Jesus made the hero a Samaritan, who was an enemy to the Jewish people. He spoke to women in public and revealed that he was the messiah to a Samaritan woman who had been married five times. Jesus illustrates by his words and actions that our love is to be like his: an inclusive love, embracing people of every race, religion, and nationality. When our ideas about people are narrow, incomplete, or false, Jesus challenges us to meet them face-to-face while listening to them with respect and understanding.

Reader   A reading of the gospel according to Luke. (Luke 10:25–37; this gospel could easily be acted out as it is read)

Pause

Reflection

This gospel reading reminds me of a story about the great entertainer Ray Charles. When he was a boy, Ray Charles was sent away to a school for the blind. But his blindness was not his greatest suffering. You see, the only piano in the orphanage sat on the "whites only" side of the building. The great genius of Ray Charles was for a time imprisoned by the prejudices and policies of the people around him. Although Ray Charles was physically blind, those who could see with their eyes held racist attitudes that left them morally blind.

Sometimes we too put people in boxes to make us feel comfortable and in control. We never let those people be themselves in our presence; they can only be the caricature we allow them to be. We put them in the prison of our minds. The story of the Good Samaritan points to the love of neighbor that Jesus expects from us. It is a love that includes those people we may have been taught to hate or fear. It is to understand that our neighbor is not only the person who lives next to us, but any person in need of our assistance. Let's continue to pray that we never put people into boxes but give them the freedom to be God's children.

Quiet Time

Response

Leader   God of all people, Jesus said our neighbor is anyone in need. But our journey through life takes place in a world where a man can be dragged behind a truck and killed because of the color of his skin, or be persecuted because of religion or sexual orientation. We pray that our love of neighbor may be inclusive, as is the love of Jesus. Together we ask God to free us from the need to discriminate against people anywhere. We pray that we may love our neighbor with the openness and generosity with which Jesus loves us.

Our response will be, "Jesus, whatever we do to the least of our brothers or sisters, we do to you."

Each pray-er will go to the place where the Book of the gospels is resting. He or she will hold it high before the prayer and say, "Holy God, your words in Scripture remind each of us that whatever we do for the least of our sisters or brothers, we do for you. And so we pray.

Pray-er One   God of love, we say we value uniqueness, the manner in which each person expresses his or her self-understanding. Help us to respect those whose self-expression is different than our own. Teach us to overcome our fear of what is strange or unusual by talking and listening to the people who challenge our narrow-mindedness and who offer us a new perspective on life. For this we pray,

All   Jesus, whatever we do for the least of our brothers or sisters, we do for

	you.
Pray-er Two	God of love, we sometimes overcome our fear and our discomfort with the unknown by putting individual people into categories. We stereo-type them according to a fixed image that denies them their personal value. Help us, loving God, to understand that no one fits into our stereotypes. Lead us to be free from stereotyping others so we can get to know that individual people are a mixture of strengths and weak-nesses, just like we are. For this we pray,
All	Jesus, whatever we do for the least of our brothers or sisters, we do for you.
Pray-er Three	Loving God, when Jesus was asked who is our neighbor, he told the story of the Good Samaritan. He showed us that our neighbor is not the person closest to us but anyone in need. Help us to grasp and prac-tice this new way of understanding who our neighbor really is. For this we pray,
All	Jesus, whatever we do for the least of our brothers or sisters, we do for you.
Leader	Loving God, you have created people who speak many languages, prac-tice many religions, have many styles of dress, and share different skin color. We pray in gratitude for this rich diversity. We want to reflect your creative love by learning to know and to accept those who look, speak, and act differently than the people with whom we usually associate. For this we pray,
All	Jesus, whatever we do for the least of our brothers or sisters, we do for you.
Leader	*Holding the Holy Scripture.* Holy God, your words in Scripture remind each of us that whatever we do for the least of our sisters or brothers, we do for you.
All	Amen.

CHAPTER 15

Freedom Isn't Free

Holy Discipline

Times for Use
- Ash Wednesday and Lent
- Thanksgiving
- Fourth of July
- Retreat theme of freedom

Introduction

Leader   Freedom is a word that we hear very often. Political freedom is celebrated on the Fourth of July. Freedom from want is one of the gifts for which the country pauses to thank God on Thanksgiving. The first European settlers came to this land seeking religious freedom and freedom of speech. What does the word "freedom" imply?

        This prayer service will begin with two reflections: on the season of Lent and the idea of freedom. There will be quiet time with music between each reflection.

Reflection One

What is freedom and how is it connected to the holy season of Lent?

| Reader One | Lent is the time when the Church invites each of us to say "no" to self-ishness. We are invited to discipline not only our desire for food, but also our desire to feel superior to others by spreading gossip. We discipline our tendency to surpass the efforts of others by cheating on a test. We say "no" to our attempts to gain popularity through buying clothes or showing off. Through our discipline we gain the freedom to control those instincts that seek to manipulate others and lead us to pretend we are someone we are not. |

Quiet Time

Reflection Two

Is freedom an escape from something or the power to love?

| Reader Two | Lent is not only a time to say "no" to the selfishness that lies within us; it is especially a time to say "yes" to those who need us most. We say "no" to being self-centered in order to become free to love the hungry and poor among us. We fast and pray that we may become more Christ-like and that the poor may benefit from our efforts. During Lent we say "no" to our selves to fight selfishness, which blocks our freedom to love others and to love God. If we want freedom, we must be disciplined. Only the truth will set us free. |

Pass out papers on which the names of well-known people—such as Tiger Woods, Meryl Streep, Madame Curie, Michael Jordon, Dorothy Day, Dr. Martin Luther King, Jr., and others—have been written. Ask those who hold the papers to name the gift for which the celebrity is known. Next, ask why the person named has the freedom to do what the average person cannot do. Emphasize that freedom is the result of asceticism, discipline in life's choices.

| Leader | You may not think of Lent as being a season for freedom. You may have heard someone say, "It's a free country, and I can do what I want." Some people see freedom as having as many choices as possible in deciding what to buy. You may have heard someone say, "I'm going to shop until I drop." Sometimes when a person is warned of the danger to health of smoking cigarettes or introducing other drugs into their body, they boast, "It's my body, I can do what I want with it." These are all familiar but mistaken understandings of freedom. Our prayer service invites each one of us to reflect on what we mean when we use the word "freedom." |

Call to Prayer

Leader   Let us remember we are in the holy presence of our loving God. Holy Spirit, you continue and complete the work begun by Jesus through the choices we make each day. We are co-creators with you in forming the world in which we live. Help us to understand the meaning of true freedom. Guide us to respect the gift of freedom that is the chief characteristic of human dignity and the mirror in which we recognize your image and likeness in our own human reflection. We pray this in union with Jesus.

All   Amen.

Scripture Reading

Leader   A reading from the gospel according to John. (John 8:31, 32)

Reflection

There was once an inmate in a state prison; we can call him Jim. He was rugged and middle-aged, and he prayed daily. Years earlier, Jim had been found guilty of a violent crime. Before sentencing, he fled from the United States to Canada. He turned his back on his wife and child, and on the people he victimized. Jim went from eastern Canada to Queen Charlotte Island on Canada's west coast. There, with a new name and a false identity, he was physically free.

One day, Jim planned to embark on a kayak trip. All was ready, but he hesitated. Jim kept thinking about what he had done, and the people he had left behind. He said it was as if his conscience was slapping him in the face. Finally, he became so tormented by his conscience and guilt over his actions that he returned back to the U.S. and turned himself in. Jim gave up his physical freedom and returned to suffer many years in a state prison.

The story of Jim's odyssey illustrates well the teaching of Jesus in John's gospel. Jim was physically free in Canada but he was morally bound by guilt over the grievous wrongs he had committed. Because he listened to his conscience, because he responded in freedom to his conscience, Jim now enjoys physical and moral freedom. Jim listened to a very painful truth, and that truth set him free.

Freedom is not about doing what we want. Freedom is about doing what is morally right.

Quiet Time

Response

A group of five young people will be invited to stand before the congregation holding a lit candle. They will be the prayers for the ceremony. After each reads his or her prayer and hears the response, they may go into the congregation to pass on the light of freedom to their peers.

Leader	Our prayer will be complete in a choral response. Our response is, "Lord Jesus, you are the light of the world. May your truth set us free."
	Liberator God, we stand holding candles that represent the light of freedom. Hear our prayers as we ask you to help us to become a free people. Lead us away from those forces in our society that promise us freedom while leading us into the enslavement of addictions. Guide us to discipline our minds, tongues, and selfish behaviors this Lent. May our fasting from food help us to know a bit more how the hungry feel each day. May we seek to love you our God by our merciful action toward them. We pray this through Christ our Lord.
All	Lord Jesus, you are the light of the world. May your truth set us free.
Pray-er One	Freedom we cry, O Lord. Teach us to think before we act and to make decisions that help us grow and respect the rights of our neighbor. As I pass on the light of freedom we pray,
All	Lord Jesus, you are the light of the world. May your truth set us free.
Pray-er Two	We pray for freedom, O Lord. Help us, Lord to know real freedom demands discipline and saying no to selfishness. May our Lenten sacrifice lead us to true freedom, we pray,
All	Lord Jesus, you are the light of the world. May your truth set us free.
Pray-er Three	We seek freedom, O Lord. Guide us each day. Help us consider the consequences of our actions. May we avoid what is evil and do what is good. With faith in your presence, we pray,
All	Lord Jesus, you are the light of the world. May your truth set us free.
Pray-er Four	We will follow the way of freedom, O Lord. Loving God, it is by following our conscience that we will become our best selves and learn to enjoy the satisfaction that comes from doing the right thing. With confidence that our choices will lead us to you, we pray,
All	Lord Jesus, you are the light of the world. May your truth set us free.

Pray-er Five	You give us freedom, O Lord. When we act in true freedom we discover your presence hidden within us. Draw us to yourself this Lent by leading us to know what is true and good. Give us the courage to choose it. With hope in your light of truth and love we pray,
All	Lord Jesus, you are the light of the world. May your truth set us free.
Leader	We extinguish our candles but we now become the light of Christ for our families and our friends. Christ, light of the world, help us to bring your light into the lives of those we meet each day.
All	Amen.

CHAPTER 16

Seeking Happiness Where It Can't Be Found

Saying "No" to Alcohol and Drugs

Times for Use
- For a Red Ribbon Day
- Before a dance or prom
- For a retreat presentation on happiness and the will of God

Introduction

Leader   The use of alcohol and drugs causes heartache in the lives of far too many young people and their families. Although it is true that young people drink to have fun, a high school senior notes a deeper reason. Do you agree with what this senior says?

Reader   "Teens today miss something. Some lack a moral code, a personally chosen set of values to guide their decisions. We have so much with which to stimulate ourselves, but we are not happy; we are bored. So kids resort to something that will make them happy fast. But, later, the problems are still there, the emptiness."

70

Leader   Boredom amid constant stimulation is a spiritual problem. Unhappiness in the midst of shopping malls and material wealth underlies a hidden emptiness and disappointment with life. Drugs and alcohol provide a quick fix for the enduring pain. They cover over the problem but never uproot it from our lives. Some questions invite a response.

Divide the teenagers into groups of five, with a facilitator for each group. Ask them to arrive at one or two answers per group and share these with the larger group. Dissenting positions may be noted. Two groups can respond to the same question.

Questions

1. Because of ignorance about the effects of alcohol and drugs, many young people are harmed. Please make a list of the biological and psychological effects of taking alcohol or specific drugs. Include long and short-term consequences.

2. Each year many young people are killed or injured in accidents directly related to alcohol or drug use. Make a list of some of the reasons that young people risk ruining their lives for the sake of a brief change in consciousness.

3. Some young people drink alcohol because it is a quick, thoughtless way to relax. Can you develop a list of other ways to have fun?

4. Alcohol and drug use is often a result of boredom. Do you see this as a spiritual problem that can be understood through greater self-knowledge and in relationships with caring people?

5. Many young people know their friends are at risk because of alcohol and drug use. If your best friend were on the way to ruining his or her life due to alcohol and drugs, what steps would you take?

6. Society gives young people mixed messages about drinking and drug use. Parties, tailgating before football games, and advertising all send negative messages, especially when the other big message out there is Just Say No. Make a list of the ways you are given mixed messages about alcohol and drug use.

After group responses are shared, continue with the prayer service.

Call to Prayer

Leader   Let us remember we are in the holy presence of a loving God.

God all merciful, you give us a free will to decide our actions and a moral conscience to guide us to right behavior. We pray for insight into the dangers of alcohol and drug use. Help us to be honest with ourselves and learn how to live happy and fulfilled lives. Guide us to think before we act in order to make good decisions based on sound knowledge. Free us, loving God, from developing ways of having fun that can only lead to dependence, broken relationships, and lives out of control. We pray for your guidance, Spirit of love, through Jesus our Lord and brother.

All   Amen.

Scripture Reading

Leader   In the Scripture reading Paul reminds us that sin is not to rule our bodies. Jesus freed our bodies from the control of sin and we are to use our bodies to glorify God. We are to be free, not enslaved by anything. God's Spirit dwells in our bodies and we will only find the happiness we seek by following the lead of the Spirit. The choices we make about food, drink, clothing, and possessions will free us to use these gifts of God in loving service to others, or it will give material goods the power to control our bodies, minds, and wills. Let's listen together to God's word.

Reader   A reading from the first letter of Paul to the Corinthians. (1 Corinthians 6:12–14, 19–20)

Pause

Reflection

After careful preparation, you may ask a student to read the following.

When I walk through the hallways of school, I realize just how big a problem drugs and alcohol really are. Especially on Friday afternoons, I can hear my classmates talking about their plans for the weekend, and most involve alcohol, drugs, or both. In our society the consumption of alcohol and drugs is glamorized all around us. It makes it increasingly more difficult for people our age to say "no" to drinking and other drugs. Some discussions in the hallways include bragging about how much someone can drink before he throws up or how many beers it takes to block any memory of what went on at the party. That is what I hear, and it points to a real problem.

Leader   Perhaps, the above look at drug and alcohol use is not your experience; perhaps it is. It *is* clear that far too many young people are seeking happiness in ways that can have lasting, destructive consequences on their lives. Alcoholism is a serious problem in this society. Problem-drinking is another. The use of other drugs enslaves the users in frightful ways. All of these destroy relationships, have a negative influence on academic achievement, limit employment opportunities, and lead to low self-esteem.

The desire for happiness is natural. God has created us for eternal joy. But many young people have no clear vision of the future consequences of their behavior. They are out of touch with the needs of their spiritual nature and are seeking happiness where it cannot be found. A way to take charge involves knowledge of the effects of drugs and alcohol, as well as choosing friends who support our values. Thinking about immediate and long-range goals, and prayer for the strength to do God's will, can lead us to take charge of our lives. We are the temple of God, each and every one of us. We can help one another to glorify God through our bodies.

Quiet Time

Response

This prayer service is a great time to pass out red ribbons as a sign that the young people will resist the social pressure to use drugs and alcohol.

Leader	Our response to God's word will be twofold. We will say together the pledge typed on the cards that are now being passed out.

One pledge is written below. Those organizing the prayer service may want to write their own pledge. The participants should be given these beforehand to know what the pledge contains. The pledge must be a free response.

All recite pledge	We recognize the danger of alcoholism, abusive drinking, and drug use in our society. We believe our bodies are temples of God's Spirit. We believe as followers of Jesus we are to glorify God by the manner in which we use our bodies. We believe that we are created by God to be free from domination by any chemical. We know we have a free will that we can use to glorify God or to make decisions that are harmful to our selves and to others. We pledge to refrain from the use of alcohol and drugs. We pledge to seek happiness in friendships, laughter, music, dance, athletics, and the art of good conversation.
Leader	We will conclude with a prayer for conviction in our refusal to use alcohol and drugs. We will pray too for healing for those who have become victims to alcohol or drug use. Our response will be, "May we glorify you, loving God."
Pray-er One	In our use of food and drink, we pray,
All	May we glorify you, loving God.
Pray-er Two	In our desire for happiness and joy, we pray,
All	May we glorify you, loving God.
Pray-er Three	In the music we hear and the videos we watch, we pray,
All	May we glorify you, loving God.
Pray-er Four	By our prayers for those addicted to alcohol and drugs, we pray,
All	May we glorify you, loving God.

Pray-er Five	By our friendship and good example with those who are tempted by alcohol and drugs, we pray,
All	May we glorify you, loving God.
Pray-er Six	In our desire to be the best people we can and to follow Jesus in doing your holy will, we pray,
All	May we glorify you, loving God.
Pray-er Seven	Creator God, you formed us in your image and likeness. Your love in Jesus saves us from the control of sin and its consequences. Your Spirit fills us with life and invites us to use all the gifts of your creation to become people who love others. Teach us to count as precious each new day and guide us to use the goods of this earth to glorify you by loving your people and this bounteous earth that sustains our lives. May we glorify you with our bodies. We pray this in the name of Jesus our Savior and brother.
All	Amen.

CHAPTER 17

Will I Live to Work, or Work to Live?

Discovering Our Vocation

Times for Use
- A day of reflection on vocation
- A retreat presentation on discernment of the future
- The feast of St. Joseph the Worker
- For the theme: my dream

Introduction

Leader   A high school senior recently said to me, "We are so wrapped up in being the best, the most popular, and, most wealthy that we forget to be happy." It does appear even in high school that many people live to work rather than work to live. The dreams of many young people are sacrificed for a job that pays more money but involves hours of tedious work. A job is something we do for money. A vocation is an answer to God's call. It is a way to live our passion, to develop and use our talents for personal growth and the improvement of the human family. We may ask, what is my dream? What are my talents, and in what career could they be generously used? What are the signs that God is calling me to follow a particular vocation? These questions are worthy of prayer and reflection.

Call to Prayer

Leader   Let us remember we are in the holy presence of a loving God. Generous Lord, you give to each of us a unique set of gifts and talents. Help us to know and to own our own abilities. Teach us how we can best use our gifts to develop all of our potential as well as serve the human community, especially those people most in need. We ask this in union with Jesus our Lord and brother, and by the power of God's Holy Spirit who now lives in our hearts.

All   Amen.

Scripture Reading

Leader   How we can know what God is calling us to do with our lives? We may be confused about what path to follow in the future years. This reading from the first Book of Samuel shows that at first, he was not aware that it was God who was calling him.

This might be an appropriate time to have other adults speak briefly to the young people about marriage, religious life, and career choices.

Reader   A reading from the book of First Samuel. (1 Samuel 3:1–10)

Pause

Reflection

A young girl could not decide what to do with her life. She was often found volunteering for special projects, such as the Special Olympics or the Aids Walk for Life or a campaign to raise awareness of homelessness. She was always involved in helping others. But when it came to selecting a career she did not know what to do.

One friend told her to choose a career that would make her financially wealthy. A guidance counselor advised her to get more schooling. A member of her soccer team told her she would make a good coach. Finally, she asked the two children whom she cared for on weekends. They looked at her with love in their eyes, and with a smile they asked, "What do you want to do? What do you *really* love—besides us?" The girl started to think about how she spent her time. She reflected on her personality, her love of people, especially young children. She became aware of her longing to do something to help those families who were financially poor. She realized that it was important to have the help of others when thinking about her future, but the call from God was within her all the time.

Sometimes people know all along what God is calling them to do with their lives. At other times though, like young Samuel, we may not know in what direction God is calling us. Then it is through family, friends, the encouragement of a parent or teacher, or an experience using one's gifts that God shines a light on our path. Let's now pray and reflect on the unique circumstances of our lives, and look for the guideposts God has left to aid us with our decisions about our future.

Quiet Time

Response

Leader	As a response to the reading we will join together in prayer that we may know the direction in which God is leading each one of us. We will use choral prayer, left and right side. Our response will be, "Help me to know my calling, Lord. Help me to choose your will."
Left Side	Spirit of Wisdom, there are many paths, which we can follow in life. Help us to discern the way that will best develop our unique gifts that will serve your people and complete your holy will. For this we pray,
All	Help me to know my calling, Lord. Help me to choose your will.
Right Side	Teacher, factory worker, computer programmer, or nurse; there are many choices of vocation. Help each of us to identify our talents and match them with the needs of people who live in our community. For this we pray,
All	Help me to know my calling, Lord. Help me to choose your will.
Left Side	Lord, there are many ways you communicate to us the vocation that is your call and challenge to us. Help us to look for signs of our calling in our family, our friends, teachers and coaches, nuns and parish priests. For this we pray,
All	Help me to know my calling, Lord. Help me to choose your will.
Right Side	Lord, Samuel did not recognize your voice. Sometimes we don't recognize you, either. Teach us through attentive listening to be open to the ways you speak to us. For this we pray,

All	Help me to know my calling, Lord. Help me to choose your will.
Left Side	Lord, you call us to use our talents to do your will, just as you called Samuel. Teach us to think carefully and to pray for your guidance before we decide on marriage, celibacy, or the religious life. For this we pray,
All	Help me to know my calling, Lord. Help me to choose your will.
Leader	Loving God, as you called Samuel so you call each of us to use our gifts, develop our talents fully, and serve your people, especially those who need us most. May we be open to your Holy Spirit in the decisions we make about our future. We ask this in Christ's name,
All	Amen.

CHAPTER 18

Will You Watch with Me?

Holy Week

Times for Use
- Holy Week
- Presentation on the mystery of human suffering
- Reconciliation service

Introduction

Leader

Have you ever been confronted with an experience that leaves you speechless? For example, people who view the Grand Canyon for the first time sit in stunned silence. Others are so overwhelmed by its presence that they cry. Sometimes there are no words to accurately describe an event, an occurence, or a person. This is the feeling of the Church during Holy Week. Attention, silence, reverence, wonder, awe, and gratitude seem to be the best ways to observe the acts of God's love that we celebrate in liturgy and prayer this week. The crucifix in the center of our gathering is a visible reminder of the love of God that fills each of us at this present moment.

Call to Prayer

Leader Let us remember we are in the holy presence of a loving God. Compassionate God, this week we wait and watch with you. We pray for a share in your way of seeing, your way of loving. Only this can free us from the fear of failure and liberate us from our relentless concern with the self. We pray in Jesus' name,

All Amen.

Scripture Reading

Leader This week the Church encourages us to reflect on the last days of Christ on earth. We often say it is hard to believe in God because we can't see God. This week we can see God in action. We can measure God's understanding of love with our own. We are invited to let go of our concerns, to become self-forgetful and to focus on the actions of our God in history. If we do this, we can get a glimpse of how God sees and how God loves.

Reader A reading from the second letter of Paul to the Corinthians. (2 Corinthians 5:5–21)

Pause

Reflection

Reader One The story of God's love for us is illustrated in a very dramatic way this week. The events celebrated are beyond description. The story told in the passion, death, and resurrection of Jesus transforms *all* of life, and extends the boundaries of human life. The story pushes our understanding of time to include the eternal. It extends our experience of the body and the material world to include the spirit. The story the Church tells this week confronts our fear of death and transforms it into hope for a share in the resurrection of Jesus Christ. This is the new life Paul describes as living for the one who died for us. This is what it means to be a new creation, to be reconciled to God and to one another.

Reader Two Each of us is also confronted this week with the mystery of suffering, both in our own lives and in the life of Christ. We don't understand the suffering of people with terminal illnesses. We don't understand the suffering of children who are victims of war, women and men who labor in sweatshops because of other people's greed, refugees who suffer hunger and homelessness on a planet rich in resources. We may become like Pilate and put God on trial. "How dare you allow such evil. How dare you let my prayer go unanswered. How dare you!"

Reader Three　　This week we remain silent and ponder life's meaning from God's perspective, God's point of view. We try to die a little to our fear, to our absorption with our self and its unending demands. This week we leave these at the foot of the cross. This week we keep silent. We watch how God loves us, how God sees us. Sometimes there are just no words.

Quiet Time

Response

Leader　　We will respond to our God by reflecting on our sins and failings. If so moved by God's Spirit, we will confess our sins and turn back to God's way of seeing, God's way of loving with all of our hearts.

Play appropriate music while the teenagers receive the sacrament of reconciliation. Cards with an examination of conscience and an act of contrition may be left in the seats. If the leader chooses, this may be reviewed orally. When all have returned from confessing, conclude the service.

Leader　　God of love, we walk with you this week the steps you took through your passion and death to the wondrous gift of resurrection. May the confessing of our sins lead us to lives of love. May we see as you see and love as you love us each day of our lives. We pray this through Christ our Lord and brother, and by the power of your Holy Spirit who lives in our hearts.

All　　Amen.

CHAPTER 19

Overcoming Obstacles

The Virtue of Hope

Times for Use
- A retreat on the Christian life
- Connecting confirmation with a deepening relationship with Christ
- Connecting the present to the future
- In time of crisis

Introduction

Leader

In the changes, conflicts, and challenges of growing up in the twenty-first century, the importance of the virtue of hope is paramount. The new millennium places new and old challenges before young people. The need to develop an authentic identity, to become sexually, emotionally, and socially mature, remains constant. Concerns about successful relationships, academic achievement, and future careers are also traditionally adolescent concerns. But these challenges will surface in the context of new and troubling events.

This millennium opens on a world fearful of terrorism. Young people today will experience the effects of global warming. They will know first hand new limits and necessary changes in lifestyle due to the diminishment of non-renewable resources. The young will face the human and

Christian challenge of sharing the earth's resources with a growing population that now numbers almost seven billion people. These challenges, along with those still to appear, will demand new vision, a well-developed faith, and constant hope in God's providence. Hope is the confident expectation of God's blessings. It does not seek to escape life's difficulties but to face them rooted in knowledge of God's love. Hope is a sign of mature faith amid the uncertainties and disappointments of life in the real world.

Call to Prayer

Leader   Let us remember we are in the holy presence of a loving God. In the name of the Creator,

All   Who places order, beauty, and truth in each created particle from the most immense to the smallest string of matter.

Leader   In the name of Jesus, the Risen One,

All   Who joins matter to spirit, earth to heaven, and human love to divine love.

Leader   In the name of the Sanctifier,

All   Who fills every corner of the universe with Godly play and purpose that love would be supreme in heaven and on earth. Amen.

Scripture Reading

Leader   Hope is the virtue or the strength in us that helps us to see the present from God's perspective. Amid the trials we face each day, hope leads us to seek God's reign, to desire eternal life, and to trust in God's Spirit working in our world. We will listen to two passages from Paul that uncover for us the beautiful virtue of hope.

Reader   A reading from the letter of Paul to the Romans. (Romans 5:3–5 and Romans 15:13)

Pause

Reflection

Story One

One tire on his wheelchair went flat when he hit the curb; the other popped when he hit a pothole, but the determined athlete finished the marathon in just over eight hours. For eight hours the man with cerebral palsy pushed himself backward in his wheelchair using only his left foot.

Story Two

He is now over fifty years old. He lies on his back paralyzed from the neck down. A car accident took away his bodily mobility but not his spirit. From his bed he celebrates his birthday with cake and candles, accompanied by the singing of some high school visitors. He smiles and responds as best he can to some of the young women. Then the party ends. Over the next few days, the man decides that he wants to do something good for other people in need. A nun from Central America informs him of her work with orphans who have AIDS. Without hesitation, he decides to become the financial sponsor of a young girl. He believes it is a good way to serve God's people.

Hope is not optimism. For the Christian, hope is trust in God's word. It is desiring God's will and asking to be guided in life by the grace of the Holy Spirit. Hope is rooted in the resurrection of Christ and the knowledge that ultimately, death in all its forms has been overcome by God's love. Hope is not rooted in our wishes, but in God's presence to us and God's action in our world.

In our two stories we learn of suffering, endurance, and hope on a human level. Without the hope of a positive outcome, obstacles would be avoided or denied but never overcome. Christian hope extends beyond our ability to bring about the desired future and trusts in God's providential care, which begins now but will only be fulfilled in the life to come. Do we live in hope, or do we try to escape obstacles that block our way in life? Do we trust in God's promise to never leave us alone, or do we seek the future in places and ways it can never be found?

Quiet Time

Response

Leader	We now join in a choral response to God's word to us. Let us pray to God whose love for us is the anchor of our hope.
Left Side	We bring our fears to your faithful presence.
Right Side	We bring our disappointments to your words of healing.
Left Side	We bring our desires to your compassionate care for us.

Right Side	We bring our confusion to your understanding presence.
Left Side	We bring our hurts and wounds to your healing touch.
Right Side	We bring our doubts to your constant faith in us.
Left Side	We bring our thirst for justice and peace to the waters of your love.
Right Side	We bring our despair to hope in your faithful love.
Left Side	We bring our fear of death to the hope in the Resurrection of Christ.
Leader	Julian of Norwich lived many years ago as an anchoress at the Cathedral of Norwich, England. In the face of the black plague and the suffering it inflicted on God's people, she expressed clearly her hope in God's ultimate victory over death. We close by making her prayer our own.
Pray-er One	We believe with Julian that,
All	All will be well.
Pray-er Two	We state our hope in her words,
All	All will be well.
Pray-er Three	Embraced by your love for us we pray,
All	All manner of things will be well.
Leader	God of Hope, you are the foundation on which we build our hope in the future. Help us to grow in knowledge of you and in the experience of your ever-present love for us. When others encourage us to see only from the perspective offered by this world, help us to include your vision of this limited life completed in the world to come. We pray this with hope in your presence and promises.
All	Amen.